RIVER CAFE
POCKET BOOKS
SALADS &
VEGETABLES

RIVER CAFE
POCKET BOOKS
SALADS &
VEGETABLES

ROSE GRAY AND RUTH ROGERS

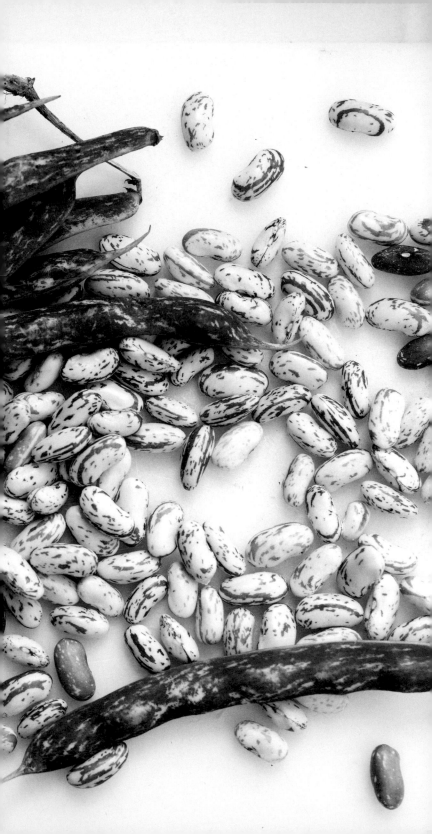

Introduction

The best vegetables come from careful and knowledgeable growers. Where and how produce is grown, when it is harvested, and how long it has taken to travel to the market, shop or restaurant, all play a part in its quality. In Italy, the region determines the variety and vegetable, and the season dictates its availability. These principles have taught us much about seasonality and regional cooking traditions. For example, we would not make a tomato and basil salad at Christmas, knowing that the ripeness of the tomato and the flavour of the basil rely on summer sunshine. Likewise, in mid-summer, braised cavolo nero in garlic with olive oil would be disappointing as the plant needs to have experienced a few severe frosts. Only then are the leaves sufficiently creamy when cooked.

At the River Cafe we enjoy talking to the vegetable growers, and encourage them to experiment with an ever-increasing diversity. We love the fact that more and more produce from the Italian, French and Spanish markets is finding its way into our shops, giving us a picture of the tremendous variety of vegetables throughout the year.

We hope this selection of recipes will introduce you to the pleasures of this inexpensive way of cooking, which is not only healthy but also delicious.

All recipes serve four unless otherwise stated. All herbs are fresh unless otherwise stated. All eggs are large, free-range, organic unless otherwise stated. Wash all fresh herbs, fruits and vegetables in cold water before use.

CHAPTER ONE
SALADS

I Fig, basil, mint and rocket salad

*6 Ripe figs, green or purple • 2 tbs Basil leaves •
2 tbs Mint leaves • 2 tbs Rocket leaves • Juice of 1
lemon • 1 tsp Traditional balsamic vinegar • Extra
virgin olive oil*

Cut off the stem of each fig, cut each one into
quarters and place in a bowl. Mix the leaves together.

Mix the lemon juice with 4 times its volume of olive
oil, then season. Drizzle a little of this dressing over
the figs, then add the remainder to the leaves. Toss.

Place the leaves on each serving plate, add the
figs, then shake a few drops of the balsamic vinegar
over each.

2 Fig, mozzarella and basil salad

*6 Ripe figs, green or purple • 4 Mozzarella balls •
2 tbs Green basil leaves • 2 tbs Purple basil leaves •
Juice of 1 lemon • Extra virgin olive oil*

Cut off the stem of each fig and cut each one into
quarters. Tear each mozzarella ball into 4 pieces.
Place the figs and mozzarella on individual serving
plates. Season and scatter over the basil.

Mix the lemon juice with 4 times its volume of
olive oil and season. Pour the dressing over each plate
and serve.

3 Toasted bread salad with tomatoes

1 Ciabatta loaf, bottom crust cut off • 500g Ripe plum tomatoes, 4 skinned, the rest left whole • 2 tbs Red wine vinegar • 2 Garlic cloves, peeled and squashed with 1 tsp sea salt • 3 tbs Basil leaves • Juice of ½ lemon • Extra virgin olive oil

Preheat the oven to 240°C/Gas Mark 9.

Tear the ciabatta lengthways into 5cm pieces, then tear the pieces lengthways again to make thinner strips of bread. Place on a baking tray, season and drizzle generously with olive oil. Bake briefly until crisp on the edges but still soft in the centre. Put in a bowl.

Cut the whole tomatoes in half and squeeze the juice and pulp over the bread, using your hands.

Mix the vinegar with the garlic, add 4 tbs of olive oil, then add to the bread. Stir to combine. Slice the skinned tomatoes lengthways and add to the bread with the basil leaves. Toss together and serve with the lemon juice poured over.

Toasted bread salad with tomatoes (Recipe 3)

4   Raw broad bean and pecorino

2kg Young broad beans in their pods • 120g Fresh pecorino, finely sliced • Juice of 1 lemon • 4 tbs Rocket leaves • 2 tbs Mint leaves • Extra virgin olive oil

Pod the beans, discarding any large ones. The beans should be no bigger than a first fingernail, green and glossy.

Put the beans in a bowl, season generously, add 2 tbs of olive oil and toss.

Mix the lemon juice with 4 times its volume of olive oil. Dress the rocket and mint leaves with this dressing. Plate individually; leaves first, then scatter over the broad beans. Place the pecorino over each salad.

5 Raw fennel and Parmesan

4 Fennel bulbs, tough outer layers removed •
100g Parmesan, finely shaved • Juice of 1 lemon •
Extra virgin olive oil

Cut the green herby tops off the fennel and chop finely. Slice the bulbs 3mm thick across. Put the fennel and tops in a bowl and season. Add 3 tbs of olive oil and the lemon juice. Toss together.

Serve with the Parmesan shavings scattered over each plateful, drizzled with olive oil.

6 Raw porcini and Parmesan

400g Firm, fresh porcini mushrooms, carefully
trimmed and wiped clean with a damp cloth •
100g Parmesan, finely shaved • 1 tbs Chopped
flat-leaf parsley • Juice of 1 lemon • 1 Dried red
chilli, crumbled • Extra virgin olive oil

Cut the porcini into thin slices through the stalk and cap. Lay the slices over each plate.

Mix the parsley with half the lemon juice and 3 tbs of olive oil. Pour this over the porcini. Scatter over the chilli and season with sea salt. Pour the remaining lemon juice over each plate. Cover each plate with Parmesan shavings and drizzle with olive oil.

---

7 Puntarelle alla romana

2 Puntarelle heads • 12 Salted anchovy fillets, cut into 1cm pieces • 1 Garlic clove, peeled and finely chopped • 1 Dried red chilli, crumbled • 1 tsp Black pepper • 4 tbs Red wine vinegar • Extra virgin olive oil

To prepare the puntarelle, fill a bowl with cold water and add ice cubes. Pull the hollow buds from the puntarelle heads. Using a small knife, slice the buds very thinly lengthways. Place in the water to crisp and curl up. This will take 1 hour.

Mix the anchovies, garlic, chilli and pepper in a small bowl and cover with the vinegar. Leave for 15 minutes and then add 6 tbs of olive oil.

Spin-dry the puntarelles. Place on a plate and spoon over the sauce.

---

8 Zucchini carpaccio

1.5kg small, firm zucchini, trimmed • Juice of 1 lemon • 4 tbs Rocket leaves • 100g Parmesan, finely shaved • Extra virgin olive oil

Slice the zucchini at an angle into rounds 2mm thick. You can use a mandoline or a Y-shaped potato peeler.

Mix the lemon juice with 5 tbs of olive oil, then season. Toss the rocket leaves with half the lemon and oil and place on individual plates. Cover with the sliced zucchini. Spoon over the remaining lemon and oil. Place Parmesan shavings over each serving.

9 Roast beetroot and fresh horseradish salad

12 Golf-ball-sized beetroot, tail and leaf stalks intact • 1/4 Fresh horseradish root, peeled • 2 Garlic cloves, peeled and cut in half • 3 tbs Red wine vinegar • 4 tbs Rocket leaves • Extra virgin olive oil

Preheat the oven to 200°C/Gas Mark 6.

Cut off the leaves 2cm from the beetroot. If they are still fresh, use in the salad. Scrub the beetroot and place on a baking tray with the garlic. Season and toss with 3 tbs of olive oil. Cover loosely with foil and bake for 20 minutes. Remove the foil, turn the beetroot round in the oil and return to the oven for a further 20 minutes, or until tender when pierced with a knife. Allow the beetroot to cool. Mix the vinegar with the same quantity of olive oil, then add salt. Cut each beetroot in half through the stalk and place on a dish. Drizzle with 2/3 of the dressing. Toss the rocket with the remainder and place amongst the beetroot. Grate over the horseradish using the fine side of the grater.

10 Cucumber and mascarpone

500g Small, firm, unwaxed cucumbers • 250g Mascarpone • Juice of 1 lemon • 2 tbs Mint leaves • 5 tbs Crème fraîche • 2 Fresh red chillies, cut in half lengthways, de-seeded and finely sliced • Extra virgin olive oil

Peel the cucumbers, cut in half lengthways and remove the seeds, if developed. Cut each half in half again lengthways.

Mix the lemon juice with 3 times its volume of olive oil, plus salt and pepper. Place the cucumber in a bowl, add the mint and the lemon juice and olive oil and toss. Combine the mascarpone with the crème fraîche and season.

Serve the cucumber with a spoonful of the mascarpone mixture and the chillies scattered over. Drizzle with olive oil.

11 Savoy cabbage and capers

1 Small Savoy cabbage, tough outer leaves discarded • 2 tbs Salted capers, rinsed of all their salt • 2 tbs Red wine vinegar • 4 tbs Chopped flat-leaf parsley • Extra virgin olive oil

Cut the cabbage in half and remove the core. Slice the cabbage very finely and put into a bowl of cold water to which you have added some ice cubes.

Leave for 15 minutes to crisp up, then spin dry.

Mix the vinegar with 4 times its volume of olive oil. Season.

Mix 2 tbs of the dressing with the capers. Put the cabbage in a bowl, scatter over the parsley, add the remaining dressing and toss well. Serve with the capers scattered over each plate.

---

12 Boiled lemon and artichoke salad

2 Thick-skinned lemons • 4 Artichokes • 100g Sea salt • 80g Blanched almonds, split into halves • 2 tbs Chopped thyme • 2 tbs Honey • Juice of 1 lemon • Extra virgin olive oil

Put the whole lemons into a small saucepan, cover with water, add the salt and bring to the boil. Cover with a lid turned upside down so the handle keeps the lemons below the surface of the water. You may have to weight the lid down, as the lemons naturally will float to the surface. Boil for 30 minutes or until the lemons are soft and the skin can be pierced easily with a fork. Drain and cool. Cook the artichokes in a separate pan of boiling water, with 1 tsp of salt, for 20 minutes, or until soft at the centre. Drain and cool.

Peel away the tough outer leaves of the artichokes, trim the stalks if they are stringy, and remove the choke if there is any. Cut into quarters, put in a bowl and season. »

« Cut the boiled lemons in half, then scoop out and discard the soft inner pulp and stringy segments. Tear the skins of each half into 2 or 3 pieces and add to the artichokes.

Heat a small frying pan, add the almonds and allow them to brown over a medium heat. Add the almonds and thyme to the artichokes and lemons. Mix the honey with the lemon juice and add 4 tbs of olive oil. Season and pour over the salad. Toss together and serve.

13 Lentil and ricotta salad

175g Castellino lentils • 250g Ricotta • 1 Garlic clove, peeled • 1 tbs Red wine vinegar • 2 tbs Chopped basil • 2 tbs Chopped mint • 2 tbs Chopped flat-leaf parsley • 1 Fresh red chilli, cut in half lengthways, de-seeded and finely chopped • Extra virgin olive oil

Rinse the lentils, then put them into a thick-bottomed pan with the garlic clove and bring to the boil. Turn the heat down and simmer for 20 minutes. Drain, removing the garlic. Add 3 tbs of olive oil and the vinegar to the lentils. Season whilst still warm. Stir in the herbs and the chilli.

Place the lentils in a large, flat serving dish. Slice the ricotta into flat pieces and place them over the lentils. Season and drizzle with olive oil.

14 Panzanella

500g Ripe plum tomatoes, or other fleshy variety, skinned • 1 Garlic clove, peeled and squashed with 1 tsp sea salt • 2 tbs Red wine vinegar • 1 Fresh red chilli, cut in half lengthways, de-seeded and finely chopped • 1 Ciabatta loaf, crusts removed • 1 Red and 1 yellow pepper, grilled and skinned (see below), then cut into quarters • 50g Salted capers, rinsed of all their salt • 10 Anchovy fillets • 2 tbs Basil leaves • Extra virgin olive oil

Cut the tomatoes in half and squeeze into a sieve over a bowl to collect the juice. Discard the seeds. Add the garlic, vinegar, chilli and 4 tbs of olive oil to the tomato juice. Season the tomato halves.

Tear the bread into 3-4cm pieces. Put into a bowl and pour over the tomato juice. The bread should be wet; add a little water if you don't have enough juice.

Arrange one layer of bread pieces in a large serving dish, scatter over a few tomatoes, pieces of pepper, some capers and anchovies. Drizzle with olive oil, then make a second layer of bread, tomatoes, peppers, capers and anchovies. Scatter the basil over the top and drizzle with more olive oil.

To skin peppers, grill them whole until black on all sides. Place in a plastic bag, seal and leave to cool. When cool, remove the blackened skin, then scrape out the seeds and fibres.

Panzanella (Recipe 14)

15   Green beans and mustard

500g Green beans, stems removed • 3 tbs Dijon mustard • 1 tbs Red wine vinegar • Juice of 1 lemon • 3 tbs Finely chopped flat-leaf parsley • Extra virgin olive oil

Cook the beans in boiling salted water until tender, then drain.

Put the mustard in a bowl. Add the vinegar and lemon juice and then slowly add 125ml olive oil until the sauce is the consistency of mayonnaise. Season.

Add the mustard sauce to the green beans and toss to combine. Add the parsley and serve whilst warm.

16   Raw artichoke salad

4 Globe artichokes, the small, oval, pointed variety, sold with stalks intact • 1 Celery heart, top ends removed • 150g Parmesan, very thinly shaved • 1 Lemon, cut into quarters • Extra virgin olive oil

Pull off the tough outer leaves of the artichokes until you get to the paler inner leaves. Cut off the top and peel the stalk. Trim the heart of any green – a Y-shaped potato peeler works well. Cut each heart in half. Scoop out any choke or bristly purple leaves.

Slice the artichoke hearts as finely as you can, one at a time, placing the slices in a bowl and immediately drizzling with olive oil. Season with salt and pepper.

Finely slice the celery heart. Add to the artichokes and toss together. Place on serving plates and cover with Parmesan shavings. Drizzle more olive oil over and serve with the lemon quarters.

17 Bread and tomato salad

½ White sourdough loaf (stale if possible), crust removed • 6 Ripe plum tomatoes, skinned • 10 Cherry tomatoes, halved and squeezed to remove juice and seeds • 1 Garlic clove, peeled • 2 tbs Red wine vinegar • 2 tbs Basil leaves • Extra virgin olive oil

Place the plum tomatoes in a food processor with the garlic, vinegar and 2 tbs of olive oil. Season, then purée until smooth.

Crumble the bread into a bowl. Add the tomato pulp and stir together to make a thick, soupy mixture.

Season the cherry tomatoes and add them to the bread mixture. Serve with the basil leaves scattered over and drizzled with olive oil.

18 Tomato and olive bruschetta

8 Plum tomatoes, halved and squeezed to remove juice and seeds • 60g Niçoise olives, stoned • 1 Dried red chilli, crumbled • 2 tbs Red wine vinegar • 2 tbs Rocket leaves • Extra virgin olive oil

Bruschetta
4 Slices of sourdough bread • 1 Garlic clove, peeled • 1 Tomato, cut in half • Extra virgin olive oil

Preheat the grill. Season the tomatoes with salt, pepper and the chilli, then add the olives and toss .

Mix the vinegar with 3 times its volume of olive oil. Add 6 tbs of this dressing to the tomatoes and mix the remainder with the rocket.

For the bruschetta, toast the bread on both sides. Rub one side lightly with the garlic clove and press the juice of the tomato into the bruschetta. Season and drizzle with olive oil.

Place the tomato mixture on each piece of bruschetta, cover with a few rocket leaves and serve.

19 Green beans, tomatoes and potatoes

250g Green beans, stems removed • 4 Plum tomatoes, skinned • 8 New potatoes, thin skins scrubbed off • 3 tbs Red wine vinegar • Extra virgin olive oil

Cook the potatoes in boiling salted water. Drain and, whilst warm, cut into quarters lengthways. Cut the tomatoes into quarters lengthways and squeeze out the seeds and juice.

Cook the beans in boiling salted water until tender, then drain. Mix together the potatoes, tomatoes and green beans.

Mix the vinegar with 4 times its volume of olive oil, then add salt and pepper. Pour this dressing over the beans, potatoes and tomatoes and gently toss together.

20 Fresh borlotti and rocket

*1.5kg Fresh borlotti beans, podded • 150g Rocket •
2 Garlic cloves, peeled • 4 Sage leaves • 3 tbs Wine
vinegar • 2 tbs Dijon mustard • Extra virgin olive oil*

Cover the beans with cold water in a thick-bottomed
pan. Add the garlic and sage. Bring to the boil, reduce
to a simmer and cook until soft. Drain, adding 2 tbs of
vinegar and 3 tbs of olive oil. Season.

Combine the remaining vinegar with the mustard. Stir
in 2 tbs of olive oil. Add half the mustard dressing to
the beans. Toss the rocket in the remainder.

Divide the leaves between the plates. Spoon over the
beans and their juices.

21   Green bean and anchovy salad

500g Green beans, stems removed • 10 Anchovy fillets, roughly chopped • 25g Capers, rinsed of all their salt • Juice of 1 lemon • 50g Niçoise olives, stoned • 2 tbs Basil leaves • Extra virgin olive oil

Cook the beans in boiling salted water until tender. Drain and season whilst warm, then add 2 tbs of olive oil.

Mix the anchovies and capers together. Stir in the lemon juice to combine. Add 2 tbs of olive oil. Add to the beans and toss. Scatter over the olives and basil.

22   Green beans and Parmesan

500g Green beans, stems removed • 75g Parmesan, freshly grated • Juice of 2 lemons • 4 tbs Rocket leaves • Extra virgin olive oil

Combine the lemon juice with 3 times its volume of olive oil, then season. Warm a medium bowl, put in the Parmesan and mix in half the dressing to form a cream.

Cook the green beans in boiling salted water until tender. Drain and add to the bowl of Parmesan. Toss to coat the beans with the mixture.

Toss the rocket with the remaining dressing, place on serving plates and put the beans on top. Drizzle with olive oil.

Green beans and Parmesan (Recipe 22)

23 Toasted bread, olives and rocket

1 Ciabatta loaf, bottom crust removed, cut into thick slices • 4 tbs Small black olives, stoned • 100g Rocket • 1 Garlic clove, peeled • 1 tbs Thyme leaves • 1 Fresh red chilli, cut in half lengthways, de-seeded and chopped • 2 tbs Red wine vinegar • Extra virgin olive oil

Preheat the oven to 220°C/Gas Mark 7.

Put the ciabatta into a roasting tin, drizzle with olive oil and roast for 5 minutes. Turn the pieces over, drizzle with more oil and bake until lightly brown and crisp on the edges. Rub the toast with the clove of garlic. Break up the toast and put it in a bowl.

Put the olives in a separate bowl with the thyme, chilli and 1 tbs of olive oil. Mix together. Combine the vinegar with 3 times its volume of olive oil. Dress the rocket leaves with half the dressing. Add to the toast with the olives. Spoon over the remaining dressing and serve while the toast is still warm.

24 Potato, caper, anchovy and rocket salad

750g New potatoes, thin skins scrubbed off • 3 tbs Salted capers, rinsed of all their salt • 12 Anchovy fillets • 4 tbs Roughly chopped rocket • Juice of 2 lemons • 2 Fresh red chillies, cut in half lengthways, de-seeded and finely sliced • Extra virgin olive oil

Lay out the anchovies, drizzle over the juice of I lemon and sprinkle with black pepper.

Cook the potatoes in boiling salted water until firm but cooked. Drain and cut in half, then in half again. Place the potatoes in a bowl and add the capers and chillies whilst still hot. Season and add I tbs of lemon juice and 4 tbs of olive oil.

Mix the remaining lemon juice with 4 times its volume of olive oil. Toss the rocket with this dressing, then stir in the potatoes. Lay the anchovies over the salad and drizzle with olive oil.

25 Mixed summer leaf salad

Sorrel • Rocket • Rocket flowers • Mâche • Baby spinach leaves • Young beetroot leaves • Basil • Fennel herb • Mint • Borage flowers • Nasturtium flowers and leaves • Red, golden and green purslane • Orache • Land cress • Small leaves from the centre of chard and chicory plants • Juice of 1 lemon • Extra virgin olive oil

Wash and spin-dry your selection of leaves, herbs and flowers.

Mix the lemon juice with 4 times its volume of olive oil, then add sea salt and black pepper.

Toss the salad with the dressing and serve immediately, as the flowers wilt very quickly.

26 Mixed winter leaf salad

Sorrel, tough stalks removed • Rocket, a mixture of large-leaf and wild • Land cress • Mâche • Sow thistle • Dandelion leaves, white stalks removed • Red chicory leaves or puntarelle leaves • Celery, tender yellow inner leaves only • Radicchio, inner leaves, shaved into thin strips • Juice of I lemon • 2 tbs Traditional balsamic vinegar • Extra virgin olive oil

Wash and spin-dry your selection of leaves.

Mix the lemon juice with 4 times its volume of olive oil, then add sea salt and black pepper.

Toss the salad with the dressing. Drizzle drops of balsamic over each serving.

Sow thistle is a wild leaf that has a bitter-sweet taste. Pick the tender shoots before the plant has flowered.

The young tender inside leaves of the wild dandelion plant are used in salads in Italy. Pick before the flowers have developed and wash very thoroughly.

Mixed winter leaf salad (Recipe 26)

CHAPTER TWO
GRILLED VEGETABLES

27 Grilled plum tomatoes with balsamic vinegar

*500g Ripe plum tomatoes, cut in half lengthways •
2 tbs Traditional balsamic vinegar • Extra virgin olive oil*

Preheat a ridged grill pan. Scatter a plate with sea salt
and black pepper. Press the cut side of each tomato
into the seasoning. Grill the tomatoes cut-side down
for 2-3 minutes, until charred. Carefully turn them
over – they will be soft. Grill briefly on the other side.

Place on a serving dish, charred-side up, and drizzle
with olive oil and drops of balsamic vinegar.

28 Grilled marinated mixed summer vegetables

*1 Aubergine, sliced 1cm thick • 3 Zucchini, sliced
lengthways 3mm thick • 1 Red and 1 yellow pepper,
grilled and skinned (see Recipe 14) • 2 Plum
tomatoes, halved and lightly squeezed to release
excess juice • 3 tbs Chopped marjoram • Juice of 1
lemon • 1 Garlic clove, peeled and crushed with 1 tsp
of sea salt • Extra virgin olive oil*

Place the aubergine and zucchini in a colander,
sprinkle with sea salt and leave for 30 minutes. Rinse
both and pat dry.

Open the peppers out and scrape away the seeds and
fibres. Divide each pepper into its natural quarters.

Preheat a ridged grill pan to very hot. Grill the aubergine on both sides until lightly brown. Press to see if they are cooked – they should be soft after about 3 minutes. Place in a large bowl.

Grill the zucchini on both sides until tender but not soft, about 2 minutes on each side. Add to the bowl.

Season the cut side of the tomatoes with sea salt and pepper. Grill the tomatoes, cut-side down, for 1-2 minutes, until just soft. Add to the bowl. Add the peppers and the marjoram.

Combine the lemon juice with 4 times its volume of olive oil and stir in the garlic. Pour this dressing over the vegetables and toss together. Add black pepper if needed.

29 Grilled marinated mixed winter vegetables

*2 Fennel bulbs, tough outer layers removed •
1 Radicchio head, outside leaves discarded • 4 Small
leeks, outside part peeled, green tops cut off • 2 tbs
Chopped thyme • Juice of 1 lemon • 1 Garlic clove,
peeled and crushed with 1 tsp sea salt • 1 tsp
Traditional balsamic vinegar • Extra virgin olive oil*

Cut the fennel into 5mm-thick slices across the bulb.
Separate the leaves of the radicchio.

Preheat a ridged grill pan to very hot. Grill the fennel
slices on both sides until tender, about 5-8 minutes.
Put in a bowl and keep warm.

Boil the leeks whole for 3 minutes in salted water,
then drain and pat dry. Cut them in half lengthways.
Season the cut side and place on the grill for 2-3
minutes. Add to the fennel.

Place the radicchio on the grill and grill very briefly,
just to wilt and lightly brown, 1-2 minutes. Add to the
fennel and leeks. Add the thyme. Combine the lemon
juice with 4 times its volume of olive oil and stir in the
garlic. Pour this dressing over the vegetables and toss.
Scatter drops of balsamic vinegar over.

30 Grilled aubergines with tomato chilli paste

2 Aubergines, sliced 5mm thick • 2 x 400g Tins of peeled plum tomatoes, drained of their juice •2 Dried red chillies, crumbed • 3 Garlic cloves, peeled and finely sliced • 1 tbs Dried oregano • 2 tbs Red wine vinegar • 3 tbs Marjoram leaves • Extra virgin olive oil

Place the aubergines in a colander and sprinkle with sea salt. Leave for 30 minutes, then rinse and pat dry.

For the tomato chilli paste, heat 2 tbs of olive oil in a thick-bottomed pan. Add the garlic and, when lightly coloured, add the dried oregano and chillies. Stir to combine. Add the tomatoes and break them up into the garlic with a spoon. Season and, when boiling, reduce the heat and simmer for 45 minutes, stirring to prevent sticking, until you have a thick paste. Remove from the pan and spread the paste onto a flat plate, then drizzle with olive oil.

Preheat a ridged grill pan. Grill the aubergine slices on both sides until they are lightly brown and soft to the bite, about 3-4 minutes.

Arrange the aubergines on a large plate and drizzle with the vinegar and some olive oil. Spread with the tomato paste and scatter the marjoram leaves over.

Grilled aubergines with tomato chilli paste (Recipe 30)

31 Grilled marinated peppers

2 Red and 2 yellow peppers, grilled and skinned (see Recipe 14), then torn lengthways into quarters • Juice of 1 lemon • 8 Anchovy fillets • 1 tsp Red wine vinegar • 50g Salted capers, rinsed of all their salt • 2 Garlic cloves, peeled and very finely sliced • 3 tbs Marjoram leaves • Bruschetta (see Recipe 18), to serve • Extra virgin olive oil

Pour the lemon juice over the anchovies and season with black pepper. Add the vinegar to the capers.

Lay the peppers over a large plate. Scatter over the capers, garlic, anchovies and marjoram. Season with black pepper and a small amount of sea salt and drizzle over some olive oil. Serve with the bruschetta.

32 Grilled marinated red and yellow summer tomatoes

500g Ripe red tomatoes (choose a large, fleshy variety), cut in half • 500g Ripe yellow tomatoes, such as Margold, cut in half • 2 tbs Thyme leaves • 2 tbs Marjoram leaves • 3 Garlic cloves, peeled and finely sliced • Extra virgin olive oil

Preheat a ridged grill pan. Chop together the thyme and marjoram leaves with the garlic slices. Put in a bowl and add 1 tsp of sea salt and 3 tbs of olive oil.

Scatter sea salt over a board. Place the tomatoes cut-side down on the salt, then place on the preheated grill, cut-side down. Grill until the cut surface seals and is charred. Turn the tomatoes over and grill briefly on the other side.

Place the tomatoes in a serving dish and scatter over the herb mixture and some black pepper. Drizzle with olive oil.

33 Grilled fennel

4 Fennel bulbs, tough outside layers and stalks removed (keep the leafy tops) • Juice of 1 lemon • 1 Dried red chilli, crumbled • Extra virgin olive oil

Preheat a ridged grill pan.

Finely chop the green herby tops of the fennel. Slice the fennel bulbs finely lengthways, so that each slice remains attached to the stalk. Grill the pieces of fennel on both sides until they have char marks but remain quite firm. Place in a bowl and season. Mix the lemon juice with 4 tbs of olive oil, add the chilli and some sea salt, mix and pour over the fennel. Add the fennel tops and toss.

34 Grilled puffballs

1kg Puffball mushrooms, peeled and cut into slices 1cm thick • 3 tbs Thyme leaves • 1 Garlic clove, peeled and finely sliced • 1 Lemon, cut into quarters • Extra virgin olive oil

Preheat a ridged grill pan. Chop the thyme leaves with the garlic, then add 1 tsp of salt and 4 tbs of olive oil. Mix together. Brush both sides of each puffball slice with the thyme mixture and leave to marinate for 15 minutes.

Grill the slices on both sides, just to char. Puffballs cook very quickly. Drizzle with olive oil and serve with the lemon quarters.

35 Grilled radicchio

2 Radicchio heads, outer leaves discarded • Juice of 1 lemon • 2 tsp Traditional balsamic vinegar • Extra virgin olive oil

Preheat a ridged grill pan. Cut the radicchio in half through the stalk, then cut each half into 8 segments through the stalk to keep the leaves attached.

Put the radicchio slices on the grill briefly, just to wilt and lightly char. Place on a serving dish. Mix the lemon juice with 3 times its volume of olive oil and season. Drizzle this mixture over the radicchio and then sprinkle over the balsamic vinegar.

36 Grilled leeks with thyme

750g Small leeks, outside peeled, green tops cut off • 3 tbs Roughly chopped thyme • 2 tbs Roughly chopped flat-leaf parsley • Juice of ½ lemon • Extra virgin olive oil

Make a cut lengthways down each leek to open up the ends. Wash in cold water. Cook in boiling salted water for 3 minutes, then drain onto kitchen paper. When cool, split completely in half lengthways.

Preheat a ridged grill pan to very hot.

Lightly season the cut side of the leeks. Grill for 1-2 minutes until lightly brown; turn over and grill the other side. Scatter over the chopped herbs and season. Squeeze over the lemon juice and drizzle with olive oil.

CHAPTER THREE
BRAISED VEGETABLES

37 Carciofi trifolati

6 Globe artichokes • I Lemon, halved • 3 Garlic cloves, peeled and finely sliced • 2 Dried red chillies, crumbled • I tbs Chopped mint • 4 tbs Chopped flat-leaf parsley • Extra virgin olive oil

Pull the tough outer leaves off the artichokes, trim the stalks and then cut off the tough tips. Continue to trim them down to the pale green heart. Cut them in half and scoop out the choke using a teaspoon. Finely slice the halves through the stalk as thinly as you can, then place in a bowl of cold water with a lemon half.

Heat 3 tbs of olive oil in a thick-bottomed pan. Remove the artichokes from the water and pat dry. Add them to the pan and fry until lightly coloured. Add the garlic and chillies and cook until soft, then turn the heat down. Add 3-4 tbs of hot water, cover with a lid and cook gently until the water has evaporated, about 10-15 minutes. Stir in the mint and parsley and season. Add olive oil and the lemon juice to serve.

The best artichoke to use for this recipe is the spiky violet (carciofi spinosi) from Sicily. It is usually the first to appear in the shops in the spring.

38 Carciofi alla romana

4 Globe artichokes, with their stalks • 3 tbs Mint leaves • 3 tbs Flat-leaf parsley leaves• 3 Garlic cloves, peeled and finely sliced • 1 Lemon, cut into quarters • Extra virgin olive oil

Tear off the tough outer leaves of the artichokes, then trim the base of the hearts with a small sharp knife or a Y-shaped potato peeler. Peel the stalks, leaving 3-4cm of stalk attached to the heart. Slice off the tops down to the tender part. Scoop out the choke using a teaspoon.

Chop the mint and parsley together with the garlic, then add salt and pepper.

Gently prise open each artichoke heart and stuff the chopped herbs into the centre and between the leaves of each. Keep 1 tbs of herbs aside.

Heat 3 tbs of olive oil in a thick-bottomed pan; choose one that the artichokes will fit in snugly, stuffed-side down. Place the artichokes in the oil and fry for 3 or 4 minutes on a medium heat. Scatter over the remaining herb mixture, then add sea salt and pepper. Add 3 tbs of hot water and cover the pan. Cook gently until the artichokes are tender and all the liquid has been absorbed, about 20 minutes. Serve with the lemon quarters.

Carciofi alla romana (Recipe 38)

39 Vignole

4 Globe artichokes • 200g Spring onions, peeled and sliced • 500g peas (podded weight), separate large from small • 500g broad beans (podded weight), separate large from small • 10 Prosciutto slices • 3 tbs Chopped mint • Bruschetta (see Recipe 18), to serve • Extra virgin olive oil

Pull the tough outer leaves off the artichokes, trim the stalks and then cut off the tough tips. Continue to trim them down to the pale green heart. Cut each in half and then into quarters. Cut away any choke.

Heat 3 tbs of olive oil in a thick-bottomed pan. Add the spring onions and fry until soft, then add the artichokes. Fry together for 5 minutes, lightly colouring them. Add the larger peas and broad beans and continue to fry for 5 minutes to coat each vegetable in the oil. Add the remaining peas and broad beans and stir to mix. Pour in 100ml hot water, just to cover the vegetables, then lay 4 or 5 slices of prosciutto over the surface. Cover and simmer gently for 30 minutes, until all the vegetables are tender. If the liquid dries out, add olive oil, not water. Season and stir in the chopped mint. Serve with the remaining prosciutto and the bruschetta.

40   Frittedda

4 Globe artichokes, with their stalks • 200g Spring onions, peeled and roughly chopped • 500g Broad beans (podded weight) • 500g Peas (podded weight) • 2 Garlic cloves, peeled and sliced • 1 tbs Chopped thyme leaves • 100ml White wine or water • 1 tbs Mint leaves • 1 tbs Chopped flat-leaf parsley • Extra virgin olive oil

Pull the tough outer leaves off the artichokes, trim the stalks and then cut off the tough tips. Continue to trim them down to the pale green heart. Cut each into eighths, cutting away any choke.

Heat 3 tbs of olive oil in a thick-bottomed pan. Add the spring onions and, when soft, add the artichokes. Fry for 5 minutes, until lightly coloured. Add the broad beans, peas, garlic and thyme and cook for 5 minutes to coat all the vegetables in the oil. Add the wine or water, just to cover the vegetables. Cover the pan, turn the heat down and cook very slowly for 20 minutes or until all the vegetables are tender. Stir in the mint and parsley and 3 tbs of olive oil. Season and serve. Frittedda is often served at room temperature.

Frittedda is a Roman dish and every cook has a slightly different recipe – this is the basic version. The proportions of each vegetable can be changed to suit the cook – fewer artichokes and more peas makes a sweeter combination.

Frittedda (Recipe 40)

41 Broad beans with prosciutto and rosemary

750g Broad beans (podded weight) • 8 Prosciutto slices • 1 Branch of fresh rosemary, tender leaves only stripped from the stem • 10 Spring garlic cloves, peeled • Extra virgin olive oil

Finely chop the rosemary. Heat 3 tbs of olive oil in a medium, thick-bottomed pan. Add the rosemary and, after 1 minute, the broad beans and garlic. Stir together and cook just to colour the garlic. Add 4 tbs of hot water or enough just to cover the beans. Lower the heat and simmer gently until the beans are tender and most of the liquid has been absorbed. Add 2 tbs of olive oil. Tear the prosciutto into 4-5cm pieces. Lay these over the beans, cover the pan and remove from the heat. Leave for 10 minutes to allow the flavours to merge. Serve at room temperature.

This is excellent served on bruschetta or with grilled calves' liver.

42 Broad beans braised in milk with sage

750g Broad beans (podded weight) • 125ml Milk • 10 Sage leaves • 10 Spring garlic cloves, peeled • 4 Slices of sourdough bread • Grated zest of 1 lemon • Extra virgin olive oil

Gently heat 3 tbs of olive oil in a medium, thick-bottomed pan. Add the broad beans and the garlic (keep back 1 clove for the bruschetta) and slowly cook until the garlic is lightly coloured. Add the sage leaves, fry briefly to combine with the beans, then add the milk. Cover the pan and simmer for 10-15 minutes, until the beans are soft and have absorbed most of the milk. Season.

Preheat the grill. Toast the bread on both sides, then rub one side with the remaining garlic. Spoon the beans and their juices over each bruschetta. Scatter over the lemon zest and serve drizzled with olive oil.

43　Peas and spring onions

750g Peas (podded weight) • 250g Spring onions, peeled and roughly chopped • 100g Unsalted butter • 10 Spring garlic cloves, peeled and sliced • 3 tbs Chopped flat-leaf parsley • Extra virgin olive oil

Gently heat a thick-bottomed frying pan. Melt the butter in it and add the spring onions. Cook gently until the onions are soft and beginning to colour. Add the peas and garlic and cook for 2-3 minutes, then stir in the parsley and 4 tbs of hot water. Cover the pan and simmer for 15 minutes. If the peas dry up, add olive oil, not water. They should be quite wet. Season and serve.

44　Green beans with tomatoes

750g Green beans, stems removed • 500g Ripe plum tomatoes, or other fleshy tomato variety, skinned • 2 Garlic cloves, peeled and sliced • 1 Dried red chilli, crumbled • 1 tbs Thyme leaves • 2 tbs Basil leaves • Extra virgin olive oil

Cut the tomatoes in half, squeeze out excess juice and seeds, then chop roughly. Chop the garlic with the thyme.

Heat 2 tbs of olive oil in a thick-bottomed pan and add the garlic, thyme and chilli. Cook for 1 minute, until soft, then add the tomatoes and 1 tsp of sea salt.

Simmer over a medium heat until you have a thick sauce, about 15 minutes.

Cook the beans in boiling salted water until tender. Drain and add to the tomato sauce. Cook together briefly, just to combine the sauce with the beans, then season and stir in the basil. Serve with olive oil drizzled over.

---

45 Aubergines with anchovies

2 Aubergines, cut into 2.5cm cubes • 6 Anchovy fillets • 2 Garlic cloves, peeled and chopped • 3 tbs Chopped flat-leaf parsley • 50g Salted capers, rinsed of all their salt and marinated in 2 tbs red wine vinegar • Extra virgin olive oil

Sprinkle the aubergine cubes with sea salt and leave in a colander to drain for 30 minutes. Rinse and pat dry.

Heat 4 tbs of olive oil in a large, thick-bottomed frying pan until almost smoking. Fry the aubergines in batches, until light brown on all sides; you may have to add more oil as you continue. Remove from the pan, using a slotted spoon, and drain on kitchen paper.

Wipe the pan clean with kitchen paper. Add 2 tbs of olive oil and heat gently. Add the garlic and, when it is soft, add the anchovies. Stir to break them up into the garlic and oil. Return the aubergines to the pan, stir to coat them, then add the parsley, capers and their vinegar. Check for seasoning and serve.

46 Zucchini trifolati

750g Zucchini, cut at an angle into slices 1.5cm thick • 2 Garlic cloves, peeled and finely sliced • 2 tbs Roughly chopped mint • 2 tbs Roughly chopped basil • Extra virgin olive oil

Heat 3 tbs of olive oil in a thick-bottomed pan. Add the zucchini and fry to a light colour. Turn the pieces over so that the zucchini are browned on each side. Add the garlic and half the mint and basil, and stir to combine. Cook until the garlic is soft, then add 3-4 tbs of hot water. Stir, scraping up the brown juices into the zucchini as they cook. When all the water is absorbed, add the remaining herbs and season.

47 Zucchini and tomato trifolati

500g Zucchini, cut in half lengthways, then cut into 2cm pieces • 300g Cherry tomatoes, halved and squeezed to remove some of their juice and seeds • 2 Garlic cloves, peeled and sliced • 2 tbs Basil leaves • Extra virgin olive oil

Heat 2 tbs of olive oil in a thick-bottomed frying pan. Add the zucchini and garlic and cook until the zucchini begin to colour. Add the tomatoes and some salt and pepper, stir well and continue cooking for 5 minutes.

Remove from the heat and add the basil. Drizzle with olive oil. Cover and sit for 10 minutes before serving.

48   Zucchini with prosciutto

750g Zucchini, trimmed • 6 Prosciutto slices •
2 Garlic cloves, peeled and sliced • 3 tbs Mint leaves •
Extra virgin olive oil

Cut the zucchini in half lengthways. Cut the lengths diagonally across into 4cm pieces.

Heat 3 tbs of olive oil in a thick-bottomed pan. Add the zucchini and fry for 2 minutes, then add the garlic and continue to fry until the zucchini and the garlic are tender and lightly browned. Remove from the heat and season. Place the mint leaves over the zucchini, cover with the prosciutto. Cover the pan with a lid and leave for 10 minutes. Toss and serve drizzled with olive oil.

49 Braised summer squashes

250g Pattypan squash, stems removed, cut into quarters • 250g Crookneck squash, stems removed, cut in half lengthways, then into 3cm lengths • 250g Slender yellow and green zucchini, cut into discs 1cm thick • 3 Garlic cloves, peeled and finely chopped • 1 Dried red chilli, crumbled • Grated zest of 1 lemon • 3 tbs Chopped flat-leaf parsley • Extra virgin olive oil

Place the squash in a colander, sprinkle with sea salt and leave for 15 minutes. Rinse and squeeze dry.

Heat 3 tbs of olive oil in a thick-bottomed pan until very hot, then add the squash and fry quickly, browning on all sides. Add the zucchini and fry for 1 minute, then add the garlic. Season and add the chilli. Turn the heat down, cover the pan with a lid and cook for 10 minutes. Remove from the heat and stir in the lemon zest and parsley. Drizzle with olive oil and serve either hot or at room temperature.

50 Aubergines and tomatoes

2 Aubergines, cut into 2.5cm cubes • 500g Plum tomatoes, skinned and roughly chopped • 2 Garlic cloves, peeled and finely sliced • 1 Dried red chilli, crumbled • 2 tbs Basil leaves • Extra virgin olive oil

Sprinkle the aubergine cubes with sea salt and leave in a colander to drain for 30 minutes. Rinse and pat dry.

Heat 2 tbs of olive oil in a medium, thick-bottomed pan. Add the garlic and fry until golden. Add the chilli and then the tomatoes with 1 tsp of sea salt. Lower the heat and simmer for 30 minutes, until you have a thick sauce. Keep warm.

Heat 5 tbs of olive oil in a large, thick-bottomed frying pan. When the oil is smoking, add the aubergines in batches and fry until golden on all sides. Drain on kitchen paper. You may have to add more oil as you continue, since the aubergines will absorb the oil as they cook.

Mix the aubergines into the tomato sauce, add the basil and check the seasoning. Serve at room temperature.

5 1 Cauliflower with fennel seeds

1 Cauliflower, divided into florets • 1 tbs Fennel seeds, ground • 2 Garlic cloves, peeled and sliced • 2 Dried red chillies, crumbled • 350g Cherry tomatoes, halved and squeezed • 2 tbs Basil leaves • Extra virgin olive oil

Heat 4 tbs of olive oil in a thick-bottomed pan. Add the garlic, chillies and fennel seeds. Cook until the garlic is soft, then add the cauliflower. Stir to combine, then lightly fry the cauliflower for 3 minutes. Add the tomatoes, 3 tbs of hot water and season. Cover the pan and cook over a low heat for 15 minutes or until the cauliflower is soft, stirring from time to time. Add the basil and serve drizzled with olive oil.

52   Caponata

1 Aubergine, cut into 2.5cm cubes • 1 Red onion, peeled and chopped • 1 Celery heart, white part only, chopped (keep a few leaves) • 2 Garlic cloves, peeled and chopped • 4 Ripe plum tomatoes, skinned, de-seeded and chopped • 2 tbs Red wine vinegar • 35g Salted capers, rinsed of all their salt • 50g Small black olives, stoned • 3 tbs Chopped flat-leaf parsley • Yolks from 2 hard-boiled eggs, roughly chopped • Extra virgin olive oil

Sprinkle the aubergine cubes with sea salt and leave in a colander to drain for 30 minutes. Rinse and pat dry.

Heat 2 tbs of olive oil in a large, thick-bottomed pan, add the onion and celery and cook over a moderate heat until soft and beginning to colour. Add the garlic and cook until soft, then stir in the tomatoes with 1 tsp of sea salt. Simmer for 30 minutes or until you have a thick sauce. Season.

In a thick-bottomed frying pan, heat 4 tbs of olive oil. When very hot, add the aubergine pieces in batches and stir-fry to brown on all sides, adding more oil if necessary. Remove with a slotted spoon and drain on kitchen paper. Add the aubergine to the tomato sauce, then add the vinegar, capers, olives and parsley. Stir to combine. Serve with the egg yolks and celery leaves scattered over.

53   Cianfotta

1 Aubergine, cut into 2.5cm cubes • 1 Red onion, peeled and sliced • 3 Garlic cloves, peeled and finely chopped • 2 Dried red chillies, crumbled • 4 Ripe plum tomatoes, skinned and chopped • 3 Waxy potatoes, peeled and cut into 2.5cm cubes • 3 tbs Red wine vinegar • 1 Red pepper, grilled and skinned (see Recipe 14), then roughly chopped • 3 tbs Chopped marjoram • Extra virgin olive oil

Sprinkle the aubergine cubes with sea salt and leave in a colander to drain for 30 minutes. Rinse and pat dry.

Heat 2 tbs of olive oil in a medium, thick-bottomed pan. Add the onion and let it soften over a medium heat. Add the garlic and chillies and cook for 4 minutes. Add the tomatoes and 1 tsp of sea salt. Simmer gently for 30 minutes, until you have a loose, fresh tomato sauce.

Cook the potatoes in a small pan of boiling salted water until tender. Drain, sprinkle with the vinegar and add to the tomatoes with the grilled pepper.

In a thick-bottomed frying pan, heat 4 tbs of olive oil. When very hot, add the aubergine in batches and stir-fry to brown on all sides, adding more oil if necessary. Remove with a slotted spoon and drain on kitchen paper. Add to the tomato and potatoes. Mix together and stir in the marjoram.

Cianfotta (Recipe 53)

54 Peppers stewed in red wine

2 Red peppers • 2 Yellow peppers • 250ml Red wine • 4 Garlic cloves, peeled and sliced • 5 Ripe plum tomatoes, skinned, de-seeded and chopped • 3 tbs Basil leaves • Extra virgin olive oil

Heat 2 tbs of olive oil in a thick-bottomed pan, add a third of the garlic and fry until light brown. Add the tomatoes and their juices with 1 tsp of sea salt. Cook over a low heat for 30 minutes, stirring to prevent sticking. Season.

Cut the peppers lengthways into quarters. Scrape away the seeds and light-coloured fibres. Cut each piece into 3.

Heat 4 tbs of olive oil in a large, thick-bottomed pan. Add the peppers and stir-fry to blister, then add the remaining garlic. Reduce the heat and cook slowly for 20 minutes or until the peppers are soft. Stir in half the wine, let it reduce for 2-3 minutes, then add half the tomato sauce. Allow the sauce to be absorbed before adding the remainder of the wine and tomato sauce. Cook for 30 minutes. Add the basil and check for seasoning. Serve drizzled with olive oil.

55 Braised cicoria

1.5kg Bitter green cicoria • 2 Garlic cloves, peeled and sliced • 1 Dried red chilli, crumbled • 1 Lemon, cut into quarters • Extra virgin olive oil

Cicoria is sold in bunches. Remove any damaged tough outer leaves. Strip the green part of the leaf away from the stalks on the good dark green leaves and discard the stalks. Keep the paler centre leaves whole.

Cook the cicoria in boiling salted water for 5-8 minutes, until tender. Drain, keeping back 2 tbs of the cooking water. Chop the cicoria into 1cm pieces.

Heat 3 tbs of olive oil in a thick-bottomed pan. Add the garlic, fry until brown, then add the chilli and stir together. Add the cicoria and the reserved cooking liquid and cook until all the liquid has been absorbed. Serve with olive oil and the lemon quarters.

56 Braised cime di rapa

1 kg Cime di rapa, tough stalks and large outside leaves discarded • 3 Garlic cloves, peeled and sliced • 2 Dried red chillies, crumbled • Extra virgin olive oil

Cook the cime di rapa in boiling salted water until tender. Drain, keeping back 2 tbs of the cooking water. Roughly chop the stalks and leaves, keeping the florets whole.

Heat 3 tbs of olive oil in a thick-bottomed pan. Add the garlic and, when brown, add the chillies. Stir in the cime di rapa and the reserved water and cook gently for 3 minutes, until the water has been absorbed. Season and serve with olive oil.

57   Carrots Dada

*650g Carrots, scrubbed and cut diagonally into
5mm slices • 8 Garlic cloves, peeled and sliced in half
lengthways • Extra virgin olive oil*

Heat 5 tbs of olive oil in a large, thick-bottomed
frying pan. Add the carrots in one layer and fry gently,
turning the pieces over as they begin to colour
and caramelise. Season as you turn the pieces and
add the garlic.

Continue to cook gently until the garlic is brown and
the carrots are tender. You may have to cook the
carrots in batches. Serve warm.

58 Braised fresh porcini and fresh cannellini

500g Porcini mushrooms, wiped with a damp cloth and sliced 5mm thick • 500g Cannellini beans in their pods, shelled • 3 Plum tomatoes, 2 skinned, de-seeded and chopped, 1 left whole • 4 Garlic cloves, 2 peeled and finely sliced, 2 peeled but left whole • 4 Sage leaves • 1 tsp Dried oregano • Extra virgin olive oil

Put the cannellini beans in a saucepan filled with cold water and add the whole tomato, the 2 whole garlic cloves and the sage leaves. Bring slowly to the boil and simmer for 35-45 minutes, until the beans are cooked. Leave the beans in half the cooking water. Remove the garlic and sage. Add 1 tsp of sea salt and 3 tbs of olive oil to the beans. Keep warm.

Heat 3 tbs of olive oil in a large, thick-bottomed frying pan, add the sliced garlic and the oregano and cook until the garlic is soft. Add the porcini and fry until lightly coloured, then add the chopped tomatoes. Stir, then cook for 5 minutes. Season and add 3-4 tbs of the bean water. Simmer gently for 15 minutes. Drain the beans and add to the porcini. Cook together to thicken and reduce any sauce. Serve warm, with roast meat.

59 Inzimino

125g Dried chickpeas, soaked in cold water for 24 hours with 1 tsp bicarbonate of soda • 3 Garlic cloves, 2 sliced, 1 peeled but left whole • 2 Dried red chillies, 1 crumbled, 1 left whole • 3 tbs Flat-leaf parsley (keep the stalks) • 400g Tin of peeled plum tomatoes, drained of half their juices • 1 Red onion, peeled and chopped • 2 Carrots, peeled and cut into 1cm pieces • 1kg Swiss chard leaves, with their stalks • 125ml White wine • Extra virgin olive oil

Drain the chickpeas and rinse in cold water, then place in a saucepan with the whole clove of garlic, the whole chilli, and the parsley stalks. Cover with cold water and bring slowly to the boil. Skim away any scum that comes to the surface, simmer for 45 minutes or until tender, then drain, keeping back 1/3 of the liquid.

Make a tomato sauce. Heat 2 tbs of olive oil in a medium, thick-bottomed pan, add the sliced garlic and allow to colour. Add the tomatoes and 1 tsp of sea salt. Break the tomatoes up in the pan and simmer gently for 30 minutes.

Gently heat 2 tbs of olive oil in a thick-bottomed pan, add the onion and carrots and cook slowly for 15 minutes to soften. Add the chilli and season. Cut the stalks from the chard leaves and trim the edges. Cut the stalks into 1cm pieces, add to the onion and carrots and continue to cook for 10 minutes. Pour in the wine and cook until reduced by half, then add the chickpeas. Cook for a further 10 minutes. Stir in the tomato sauce.

Cook the chard leaves in boiling salted water until tender, then drain and roughly chop. Add to the chickpeas. Add the parsley and check for seasoning. Serve drizzled with olive oil.

60 Swiss chard and their stalks with chilli and parsley

1.5kg Swiss chard leaves, with their stalks • 1 Dried red chilli, crumbled • 3 tbs Chopped flat-leaf parsley • 3 Garlic cloves, 2 peeled and finely sliced, 1 peeled but left whole • Extra virgin olive oil

Cut the stalks from the chard leaves, trim the edges and cut each stalk across the grain into 2cm pieces.

Cook the leaves in boiling salted water until tender, remove from the pan and chop roughly. Add the whole garlic clove to the pan and bring the water back to the boil. Test for saltiness, then add the stalks. Cook for 6 minutes, then drain.

Heat 3 tbs of olive oil in a thick-bottomed pan, add the sliced garlic and fry until golden. Add the chard stalks, chilli and season. Stir the stalks around the pan to absorb the flavours. Add the parsley and continue to fry for 1 minute. Remove from the heat and add the chard leaves. Toss together and serve warm.

61 Erbette saltate

300g Swiss chard, leaves only or Large leaf spinach, stalks discarded • 300g Rocket • 300g Cime di rapa, prepared (see recipe 56) • 300g Bitter green cicoria, prepared (see recipe 55) • 3 Garlic cloves, peeled and finely sliced • 1 tsp Fennel seeds • 2 Dried red chillies, crumbled • Extra virgin olive oil

Cook the greens separately in boiling salted water. Cook the chard or spinach first; it will take 3 minutes. Remove with a slotted spoon and drain. Cook the rocket next, for 3 minutes. Remove and drain. Cook the cime di rapa – you may have to add more salt and water to the pot – for 8 minutes or until tender. Remove and drain. Finally cook the cicoria for 10 minutes or until tender, then drain. Chop all the greens together, keeping them quite moist.

Heat 4 tbs of olive oil in a large, heavy-based frying pan and add the garlic. Fry until golden, then add the fennel seeds and chillies and season the mixture. Add the mixed greens to the pan, stir to combine, and cook for 3 minutes. Serve drizzled with olive oil.

62 Fennel with tomato and chilli

6 Fennel bulbs, tough outside layers and stalks removed (keep the leafy tops) • 400g Tin of peeled plum tomatoes, drained of their juices and chopped in the tin • 2 Dried red chillies, crumbled • 4 Garlic cloves, peeled and sliced • 1 tsp Fennel seeds, crushed • Juice of 1 lemon • Extra virgin olive oil

Cut the fennel bulbs in half through the top and then each half into 6.

Heat 3 tbs of olive oil in a medium, thick-bottomed pan. Add the fennel and, after 2 minutes, the garlic. Add the chillies, fennel seeds and some sea salt and pepper. Fry for 5-6 minutes, stirring to combine the seasoning with the fennel, then add the tomatoes and cover with a lid. Turn the heat down and cook gently until the fennel is soft and the tomatoes have reduced to a sauce.

Chop the leafy tops of the fennel and add to the mixture. Stir in the lemon juice and 2 tbs of olive oil.

63 Slow-cooked fennel

6 Fennel bulbs, tough outside layers and stalks removed (keep the leafy tops) • 4 Garlic cloves, peeled and cut in half lengthwuys • Extra virgin olive oil

Cut each fennel bulb in half from top to bottom, then each half into 4. Heat 4 tbs of olive oil in a thick-bottomed pan. Add the fennel pieces and fry over a high heat, stirring from time to time, until they begin to brown. Add the garlic and continue frying for 2 minutes. Add 3 tbs of hot water and season. Cover the pan, turn the heat down, and cook until the fennel is tender and all the liquid has been absorbed. Remove from the heat, add the fennel tops and drizzle with olive oil.

Slow-cooked fennel (Recipe 63)

64 Braised cavolo nero

*1.5kg Cavolo nero, centre stalks stripped out •
3 Garlic cloves, peeled and finely sliced • 1 tsp
Fennel seeds, crushed • 1 Dried red chilli, crumbled •
Extra virgin olive oil*

Cook the cavolo nero in boiling salted water until tender – about 8 minutes – drain and roughly chop.

Heat 3 tbs of olive oil in a thick-bottomed pan. Add the garlic and fry until brown. Immediately add the fennel seeds and chilli, then stir in the cavolo. Season and stir over the heat for 5 minutes. Serve drizzled with olive oil.

65 Braised field and wild mushrooms

*750g Flat field mushrooms, peeled and sliced 5mm
thick • 25g Dried porcini mushrooms, soaked in
150ml hot water for 15-20 minutes • 3 Garlic cloves,
peeled and finely sliced • 1 Dried red chilli, crumbled •
3 tbs Chopped flat-leaf parsley • 1 tbs lemon juice •
Extra virgin olive oil*

Heat 4 tbs of olive oil in a thick-bottomed pan until smoking. Add the field mushrooms and the garlic and fry for 10 minutes or until the mushrooms begin to darken. Season and add the chilli.

Drain the porcini, retaining the liquid. Rinse them in a sieve under a running tap to remove any grit, then cut off any hard bits. Strain the liquid through a sieve lined with kitchen paper. Add the porcini to the field mushrooms. Fry together, adding 3 or 4 tbs of the soaking liquid. Cook until all the mushrooms are dark and moist. Add more liquid if too dry.

Check the seasoning and stir in the parsley. Add 1 tbs of olive oil and the lemon juice. Serve with grilled meats or bruschetta (see Recipe 18).

CHAPTER FOUR
ROASTED & BAKED VEGETABLES

66 Artichokes baked in foil with thyme

8 Globe artichokes • 3 tbs Thyme leaves • I Lemon, cut into quarters, plus ½ lemon for rubbing the cut artichokes • 3 Garlic cloves, peeled and finely sliced • Extra virgin olive oil

Preheat the oven to 220°C/Gas Mark 7.

To prepare the artichokes, trim the stalks to 3cm from the base, then peel off the fibres from the stalks until you get to the pale core. Tear off the tough outer leaves and trim the remaining leaves down to the paler centre of the artichoke. Cut off the top tips, then peel around the base. Pull the remaining leaves open and scoop out the choke, if any. Rub the lemon half over each artichoke to prevent discoloration.

Push slivers of garlic, thyme, sea salt and black pepper between the leaves and in the centre of the artichokes. Lay each artichoke on a piece of foil large enough to wrap around. Drizzle with olive oil, scatter sea salt over and wrap up tightly.

Roast in the preheated oven for 30 minutes. Serve with the lemon quarters and some olive oil.

67 Roast asparagus

*1.5kg Asparagus, tough ends snapped off •
3 tbs Thyme leaves • 50g Small black olives, stoned •
Juice of 1 lemon • Extra virgin olive oil*

Preheat the oven to 220°C/Gas Mark 7.

Heat 2 tbs of olive oil in a roasting tin. Add the
asparagus, thyme leaves and olives and toss to
combine. Season, then bake for 4 minutes if the
asparagus is thin, 5-6 minutes if it is fatter.

Remove from the oven and dress with lemon juice
and olive oil.

68 Slow-roast cherry tomatoes

*600g Cherry tomatoes, pricked with a fork • 4 Garlic
cloves, peeled and cut in half lengthways • 1 tbs Dried
oregano • Extra virgin olive oil*

Preheat the oven to 120°C/Gas Mark ½.

Put the tomatoes, garlic and oregano in a baking dish
with 3 tbs of olive oil and season. Place in the
preheated oven and roast for 1 hour, or until soft but
still whole.

*Slow-roast cherry tomatoes mixed with roast asparagus
(see Recipe 67) make a delicious antipasto served with
bruschetta (see Recipe 18).*

Roast asparagus (Recipe 67) and Slow-roast cherry tomatoes (Recipe 68)

69 Roast carrots

*500g Summer carrots, sold with their leaves intact •
8 Spring garlic cloves, peeled • 4 tbs Thyme leaves •
Extra virgin olive oil*

Preheat the oven to 200°C/Gas Mark 6.

Cut the leaves from the carrots, 5cm from the top.
Scrub the carrots. Place them in an ovenproof dish,
add the garlic and thyme, then season generously
with sea salt and pepper. Drizzle over 4 tbs of olive
oil. Add 100ml water to the dish.

Place the carrots in the preheated oven and roast for
20 minutes. Turn them over and continue to roast for
10 minutes or until tender.

70 Roast beetroot

*12 Golf-ball-sized beetroot, leaves trimmed to 2cm from
the top, tail kept intact • 4 tbs Thyme leaves • 4 Garlic
cloves, peeled and cut in half • Extra virgin olive oil*

Preheat the oven to 200°C/Gas Mark 6.

Scrub the beetroot and put them in a bowl. Add the
thyme, salt, pepper and garlic. Stir in 4 tbs of olive oil
and toss to coat the beetroot.

Place on a baking tray, cover with a piece of foil and
bake for 20 minutes. Remove the foil, turn the
beetroot over and roast for a further 20 minutes or
until they are tender.

71 Oven-dried plum tomatoes

12 Plum tomatoes, skinned • 3 tbs Chopped marjoram • Extra virgin olive oil

Preheat the oven to its lowest setting.

Brush a baking tray with olive oil. Place the tomatoes in it side by side, season with sea salt and drizzle with olive oil. Bake in the low oven for about 2½ hours, gently pressing the tomatoes to release their juices every ½ hour. When the tomatoes have become flat and concentrated, they are ready.

Serve at room temperature, sprinkled with the marjoram and drizzled with olive oil.

72 Roast aubergines

2 Aubergines, sliced into discs 1.5cm thick • 2 Garlic cloves, peeled and very finely chopped • 2 tbs Dried oregano • 1 Dried red chilli, crumbled • 2 tbs Red wine vinegar • Extra virgin olive oil

Preheat the oven to 220°C/Gas Mark 7.

Lay the aubergine slices in a colander and sprinkle with sea salt. Leave for 15 minutes, then rinse and pat dry.

Mix the garlic with the oregano and add 3 tbs of olive oil. Season with sea salt and pepper, then stir in the chilli.

Brush a baking tray with olive oil. Place the aubergine slices in the tray in a single layer and spread a thin amount of the garlic oil over each one. Bake for 15 minutes. Turn the aubergines over and bake for a further 10 minutes, until soft and lightly browned. Serve sprinkled with the vinegar.

73 Roast aubergines with tomatoes and Parmesan

2 Aubergines, sliced into discs 2cm thick • 8 Plum tomatoes, halved and squeezed to remove juice and seeds • 100g Parmesan, freshly grated • 2 tbs Torn basil leaves • Extra virgin olive oil

Preheat the oven to 200°C/Gas Mark 6.

Place the aubergines in a colander and sprinkle with sea salt. Leave for 15 minutes, then rinse and pat dry.

Chop the tomatoes into small pieces and put them in a bowl. Add the Parmesan and basil and season with sea salt and pepper. Stir in 1 tbs of olive oil.

Brush a baking tray with olive oil. Place the aubergines on the tray in a single layer, brush with olive oil and season. Bake in the preheated oven for 15 minutes. Turn over and spoon the tomato mixture on top. Return to the oven for 5 minutes. Serve warm.

74 Roast zucchini

12 Small zucchini, trimmed and cut in half lengthways • 4 Garlic cloves, peeled and crushed with 1 tsp sea salt • 4 tbs Finely chopped marjoram • Extra virgin olive oil

Preheat the oven to 220°C/Gas Mark 7.

Mix the garlic and marjoram together and add 1 tbs of olive oil. Arrange the zucchini cut-side up in a roasting tray. Spoon a little of the herb mixture over each. Season and drizzle with olive oil. Roast in the preheated oven for 10-15 minutes or until soft but not brown.

Roast zucchini (Recipe 74)

75 Roast marinated peppers

2 Red peppers • 2 Yellow peppers • 50g Salted capers, rinsed of all their salt, then marinated in 2 tbs red wine vinegar • 3 tbs Chopped marjoram • Extra virgin olive oil

Preheat the oven to 200°C/Gas Mark 6.

Brush the peppers with olive oil, place on a baking tray and scatter with sea salt. Bake in the preheated oven until they begin to blister. Turn them over and continue to bake until they are soft, their juices are running and their skins are blistered all over. Remove the peppers to a bowl, cover tightly with cling film and leave to cool.

When cool enough to handle, open the peppers up, peel off the skin and scrape away the seeds and fibres. Divide the peppers into quarters. Lay them on a serving plate, skinned-side up. Season with sea salt and pepper. Scatter over the capers and their vinegar. Drizzle with olive oil and sprinkle over the marjoram.

76 Roast stuffed peppers

4 Red peppers, cut in half through the stalk • 3 Garlic cloves, peeled and finely sliced • 100g Small black olives, stoned • 1 Fresh red chilli, cut in half lengthways, de-seeded and finely sliced • 2 tbs Chopped flat-leaf parsley • 100g Rocket, roughly chopped • 1 tbs Red wine vinegar • Extra virgin olive oil

Preheat the oven to 180°C/Gas Mark 4.

Scrape out the seeds and fibres from inside each pepper. Lightly oil a baking tray and place the peppers on it, cut-side up. Scatter a few slices of garlic in each pepper half and season. Sprinkle 3 tbs of water over the peppers and drizzle with olive oil. Cover loosely with a sheet of foil and bake for 30 minutes. Remove the foil and drizzle with more oil. Reduce the oven temperature to 120°C/Gas Mark ½. Return the peppers to the oven and roast until they are soft and beginning to collapse, 15-20 minutes. Cool.

Mix the olives with the chilli and parsley, then add 1 tbs of olive oil.

Dress the rocket with the vinegar and 3 tbs of olive oil. Season. Stuff each pepper half with the rocket and spoon over the olives.

77 Borlotti with roast sweet potato

1kg Fresh borlotti beans, podded • 500g Sweet potatoes, peeled and cut into 3cm pieces • 2 Garlic cloves, peeled • 1 tbs Sage leaves • 1 Plum tomato • 1 Dried red chilli, crumbled • 1 tbs Dried oregano • Extra virgin olive oil

Preheat the oven to 200°C/Gas Mark 6.

Put the beans in a thick-bottomed saucepan, cover with cold water and add the garlic, sage and whole tomato. Bring to the boil and simmer for 30 minutes or until the beans are soft.

Put the sweet potatoes in a bowl with the chilli, oregano and 3 tbs of olive oil. Season and toss. Place a piece of foil on a baking tray and arrange the sweet potatoes on it in one layer. Bake for 20 minutes, then turn the pieces over and bake until tender and crisp on the edges. Keep warm.

Drain the borlotti beans and remove the garlic, sage and tomato skin. Return the beans to the saucepan and add 3 tbs of olive oil. Cook briefly, just to give the beans extra colour. Season. Mix the beans and sweet potato together. Serve warm.

78 Baked peppers stuffed with tomatoes and anchovies

2 Red peppers, cut in half through the stalk • 2 Yellow peppers, cut in half through the stalk • 16 Cherry tomatoes, halved and squeezed to remove juice and seeds • 8 Anchovy fillets • 4 Garlic cloves, peeled and finely sliced • 50g Salted capers, rinsed of all their salt, then marinated in 2 tbs red wine vinegar • 1 tbs Red wine vinegar • 2 tbs Basil leaves • Extra virgin olive oil

Preheat the oven to 180°C/Gas Mark 4.

Scrape out the seeds and fibres from the peppers. Place them in a baking tray, cut-side up. Put a few tomatoes, slivers of garlic, an anchovy fillet and 1 tbs of capers in each pepper half with a few drops of vinegar. Season each pepper and drizzle with olive oil. Lightly cover with foil.

Bake for 30 minutes, then remove the foil and lower the oven temperature to 150°C/Gas Mark 2. Bake for a further 30 minutes, or until the peppers are soft.

Remove from the oven and place the peppers on a serving dish. Stuff a few basil leaves into each one, drizzle with olive oil and serve at room temperature.

Baked peppers stuffed with tomatoes and anchovies (Recipe 78)

79 Baked fresh borlotti

1.5kg Fresh borlotti beans (podded weight, about 500g) • ½ Spring garlic head, kept whole • 3 Tomatoes, cut in half • 3 Sage leaves • Extra virgin olive oil

Preheat the oven to 200°C/Gas Mark 6.

Put the podded borlotti beans in a baking dish with the garlic, tomatoes and sage and cover with cold water. Pour in enough olive oil to cover the surface of the water. Seal tightly with foil. Make a small hole in the centre with a sharp knife.

Bake in the preheated oven for 45 minutes or until the beans are soft, most of the water has evaporated, and the oil has been absorbed by the beans.

Drain off excess water, then remove the garlic, sage and tomato skin. Season with sea salt and black pepper. Serve drizzled with olive oil.

80 Baked dried cannellini

250g Dried cannellini beans, soaked in cold water for 12 hours with 1 tsp bicarbonate of soda • 400g Tin of peeled plum tomatoes, drained of their juices • ½ Celery head, white heart only • 4 Garlic cloves, peeled • 1 Fresh red chilli, de-seeded and cut in half lengthways • 2 Sage leaves • Extra virgin olive oil

Preheat the oven to 200°C/Gas Mark 6.

Drain the beans and rinse well. Place in a baking dish 4cm deep. Arrange the tomatoes, celery heart, garlic cloves, chilli and sage amongst the beans. Add enough water just to cover, then pour over 4 tbs of olive oil. Tightly cover the baking dish with foil and place in the oven. Bake for 45 minutes. Test for softness.

Remove the sage and mash up the celery and tomato into the beans. Drain off most of the remaining liquid. Season and stir in 3 tbs of olive oil. Serve warm.

81 Roast onion squash

*1.5kg Onion squash, stalk removed and skin scrubbed •
4 Garlic cloves, peeled and cut in half lengthways •
2 tbs Fennel seeds, crushed • 2 Dried red chillies,
crumbled • 1 tbs Dried oregano • Extra virgin olive oil*

Preheat the oven to 200°C/Gas Mark 6.

Cut the onion squash in half through the stalk end and scrape out the seeds and fibres. Cut each half into 8 boat-shaped pieces.

Put the onion squash in a large bowl and add the garlic, fennel seeds, chillies and oregano. Add 4 tbs of olive oil and season. Toss together to coat each piece with the herbs. Place on a baking tray lined with foil. Drizzle with olive oil and bake for 20 minutes. Turn the pieces over and continue to bake until soft, but crisp on the edges.

82 Baked onion squash stuffed with potatoes

2 Small onion squash, skin scrubbed • 500g Waxy potatoes, peeled and cut into 2.5cm cubes • 2 Dried chillies, crumbled • 2 tbs Thyme leaves • 4 Garlic cloves, peeled and finely chopped • 150g Pancetta, cut into matchsticks • Extra virgin olive oil

Preheat the oven to 200°C/Gas Mark 6.

Cut off the top quarter of each squash with the stem and discard. Scoop out the seeds and fibres and season the inside with sea salt, black pepper and the chillies. Put the squash on a baking tray lined with foil and drizzle with olive oil inside and out. Bake for 20 minutes.

Cook the potatoes in boiling salted water for 8 minutes. Drain, place in a bowl, then add the thyme, garlic and pancetta. Season and toss.

Spoon the potato mixture into the part-baked squash and return to the oven for a further 30 minutes, or until the squash are soft. Test by sticking a skewer into the side.

83 Roast butternut squash

1.5kg Butternut squash • 2 Garlic cloves, peeled and cut in half lengthways • 2 tbs Thyme leaves • 1 Dried red chilli, crumbled • Extra virgin olive oil

Preheat the oven to 200°C/Gas Mark 6.

Peel the squash. Butternut skin is hard, so needs to be peeled away completely. Cut the narrow end of the butternut into discs 1.5cm thick. Cut in half the other part, which is filled with seeds. Scrape out the seeds and fibres. Cut this part into 4 pieces, approximately the same thickness as the discs. Put the pieces of butternut in a bowl, add the garlic, thyme, chilli and 3 tbs of olive oil. Toss together and season. Place on a baking tray and bake for 20 minutes. Turn the pieces over and continue to bake for 10 minutes, or until the butternut is soft, and crisp and brown on the edges.

84 Roast summer squash

1kg Pattypan or crookneck squash, stems removed and cut into quarters • 500g Mixed round and long yellow and green zucchini • 2 Garlic cloves, peeled and halved • 3 tbs Chopped marjoram • Juice of 1 lemon • Extra virgin olive oil

Preheat the oven to 200°C/Gas Mark 6.

Place the squash and zucchini in a bowl. Add the garlic and half the marjoram and 3 tbs of olive oil. Season generously and toss together to coat each piece.

Place the squash and zucchini cut-side up on a flat baking tray and roast for 15-20 minutes or until the cut part is light brown. Place in a serving dish, and add olive oil, the lemon juice and the remaining marjoram. Toss to serve.

85 Roast potatoes in a saucepan

*750g Waxy potatoes, peeled and cut into 2cm cubes •
2 tbs Chopped rosemary • 4 Garlic cloves, peeled and
cut in half lengthways • Extra virgin olive oil*

Rinse the potatoes in cold water to get rid of the
starch, then pat dry. Heat a medium, thick-bottomed
pan with a lid. Pour in sufficient olive oil to cover the
bottom. When the oil is very hot, add the potatoes,
rosemary and garlic, then season and cover the pan.

Cook over a medium heat, shaking the pan to prevent
the potatoes sticking. After 10 minutes, turn the
potato pieces over to brown on the other side, cover
again and cook for a further 10 minutes.

86 Roast potatoes and lemons

*750g Waxy potatoes, scrubbed and cut into
quarters lengthways • 2 Thick-skinned lemons, stalks
and tips removed • 4 Garlic cloves, peeled and cut
in half lengthways • 3 tbs Marjoram leaves • Extra
virgin olive oil*

Preheat the oven to 220°C/Gas Mark 7.

Cut the lemons in half lengthways, then each half into
3 lengthways, then each piece in half across.

Put the potatoes and lemons in a bowl. Mix, squeezing
the juice out of the lemons with your hands into the
bowl. Add the garlic, marjoram and some sea salt and

pepper. Pour 4 tbs of olive oil over and place in an ovenproof dish. Place in the oven and roast for 30 minutes, turning the potatoes and lemons over so that they are brown and crisp on all sides.

87 Roast potatoes with spring onions, thyme and balsamic vinegar

750g Waxy potatoes, peeled and cut in half lengthways, then in half again • 350g Large spring onions, peeled and thickly sliced • 3 tbs Thyme leaves • 5 tbs Balsamic vinegar • 225g Unsalted butter • Extra virgin olive oil

Preheat the oven to 200°C/Gas Mark 6.

Melt the butter in a large casserole or roasting tin. Add the potatoes and onions, shaking the pan to coat them with the butter, and fry for 10-15 minutes until they have started to colour. Add the thyme and season. Stir in half the balsamic vinegar.

Cover with foil and bake in the oven for 20 minutes. Remove the foil, stir the potatoes to turn them over, then add the remaining balsamic vinegar and drizzle with a little olive oil. Return to the oven uncovered. Bake for a further 20-30 minutes or until the potatoes are soft and the onion has caramelised. The potatoes should take on the colour of the vinegar, and be crisp on the edges.

Roast potatoes with spring onions, thyme and balsamic vinegar (Recipe 87)

88 Roast potatoes with dried porcini and thyme

750g Waxy potatoes, peeled and sliced 3mm thick •
50g Dried porcini mushrooms, soaked in 150ml hot
water for 15 minutes • 3 tbs Thyme leaves • 100g
Unsalted butter • 4 Garlic cloves, peeled and sliced •
Extra virgin olive oil

Preheat the oven to 200°C/Gas Mark 6.

Drain the porcini, retaining the soaking liquid. Rinse in a sieve under a running tap to remove any grit. Strain the liquid through a sieve lined with kitchen paper.

Wash the potato slices in cold water and pat dry. Heat 2 tbs of olive oil with the butter in a thick-bottomed frying pan. Add the garlic, let it soften, then add the porcini. Stir together and cook for 5 minutes. Add half the reserved soaking water and simmer. Add more as it is absorbed by the porcini. Continue until you have a wet sauce. Season. Add the potatoes and continue to cook until most of the liquid has been absorbed.

Place in a roasting tin, scatter over the thyme and drizzle generously with olive oil. Bake in the preheated oven for 30 minutes, until the potatoes are browned and crisp in parts.

89 Roast potatoes with fennel and porcini

500g Waxy potatoes, peeled and cut into quarters lengthways • 500g Fennel bulbs, tough outer layers and stalks removed • 30g Dried porcini mushrooms, soaked in 120ml hot water for 15 minutes • 4 Garlic cloves, 2 peeled and sliced, 2 peeled but left whole • Extra virgin olive oil

Preheat the oven to 200°C/Gas Mark 6.

Drain the porcini, retaining the soaking liquid. Rinse in a sieve under a running tap to remove any grit. Strain the liquid through a sieve lined with kitchen paper.

Heat 2 tbs of olive oil in a thick-bottomed frying pan, add the porcini and the sliced garlic and fry gently until beginning to brown. Season and pour in half the reserved soaking water. Simmer for 15 minutes, adding more water as it becomes absorbed. Remove from the heat when the porcini are soft and the mixture is still quite liquid.

Cut each fennel bulb into 8 slices. Cook the potatoes in boiling salted water for 8 minutes. Remove from the pan with a slotted spoon and add to the porcini. Put the 2 whole garlic cloves into the boiling water, add the fennel slices and cook for 6 minutes. Drain and stir into the potato and porcini mixture. Season and add 3 tbs of olive oil. Mix well together.

Place the potato mixture in a baking dish and bake for 30 minutes or until the potatoes and fennel are soft. Serve hot, drizzled with olive oil.

Roast potatoes with fennel and porcini (Recipe 89)

90 Fresh porcini baked over potatoes

1 kg Fresh porcini mushrooms, wiped clean with a damp cloth • 500g Waxy potatoes, peeled and sliced 5mm thick • 4 Garlic cloves, peeled and finely sliced • 3 tbs Roughly torn basil leaves • Extra virgin olive oil

Preheat the oven to 200°C/Gas Mark 6.

Rinse the potato slices in cold water and pat dry. Trim the porcini stalks, keeping the caps attached where possible. Cut the porcini caps and stalks lengthways into slices the same thickness as the potatoes.

Put the potato slices in a bowl with the garlic and half the basil and season. Add 2 tbs of olive oil and toss together.

Place the potatoes in layers in an ovenproof dish or cake tin at least 4cm deep. Place the porcini slices over the potato, then scatter them with sea salt and the remaining basil. Pour 3 tbs of olive oil over. Cover with foil, seal tightly and bake for 45 minutes.

91 Roast porcini caps and stalks

750g Fresh porcini mushrooms, wiped clean with a damp cloth • 1 Lemon, cut into quarters • Extra virgin olive oil

Preheat the oven to 220°C/Gas Mark 7.

Cut the caps from the mushroom stalks. Peel and trim the stalks, then cut each stalk in half lengthways. Lay the caps, sponge-side up, on a baking tray with the stalks and season with sea salt and black pepper. Drizzle with olive oil and roast for 10 minutes or until the porcini are tender and browned. Serve with the lemon quarters.

92 Porcini baked in foil with Italian wild mint

750g Fresh porcini mushrooms, wiped clean with a damp cloth • 3 tbs Chopped nepitella (Italian wild mint), or mint and oregano • 3 Garlic cloves, peeled and finely sliced • Bruschetta (see Recipe 18), to serve • 1 Lemon, cut into quarters • Extra virgin olive oil

Preheat the oven to 220°C/Gas Mark 7.

Trim the stalks of the porcini. Cut them lengthways through the caps and stems into slices 1cm thick.

Tear some foil into four 25cm squares. Lightly brush each piece with olive oil. Divide the porcini slices between the squares of foil and cover with a few slices of garlic. Season with sea salt and black pepper, scatter over the nepitella and drizzle with olive oil. Fold the foil over to form an envelope and seal on all sides.

Place the packets on a flat baking tray. Bake in the oven for 15 minutes or until the envelopes puff up. Serve the packets at the table, with the bruschetta and lemon quarters.

Porcini baked in foil with Italian wild mint (Recipe 92)

93 Roast whole fresh porcini with pancetta and thyme

4 Large, firm fresh porcini mushrooms, with their stalks attached • 8 Thin slices of pancetta • 8 Thyme sprigs • 4 Garlic cloves, peeled and finely sliced • 1 Lemon, cut into quarters • Extra virgin olive oil

Preheat the oven to 220°C/Gas Mark 7.

Wipe the porcini caps with a damp cloth and trim the stalks of any rough bits. With a small knife, make 2 cuts up the length of the stalk, dividing it into 3, keeping the cap intact.

In each cut, place a sprig of thyme and a few slices of garlic. Wind a slice of pancetta through and around the stalks. Season the mushrooms all over.

Heat a flat oven tray and brush with olive oil. Place the porcini on the tray and drizzle with olive oil. Place the remaining pancetta loosely over the top and roast until the porcini are browned and soft and the pancetta is crisp, about 10-15 minutes. Serve with the lemon quarters.

94 Roast celeriac with butternut squash, fennel and tomato

250g Celeriac, peeled and cut into slices 2cm thick • 250g Butternut squash, peeled, de-seeded and cut into slices 2cm thick • 2 Fennel bulbs, tough outer layers and stalks removed • 4 Plum tomatoes, halved • 4 Garlic cloves, peeled and halved • Extra virgin olive oil

Preheat the oven to 200°C/Gas Mark 6.

Cut each fennel bulb lengthways through the stalk into 8 slices. Cook the celeriac and fennel in boiling salted water for 5 minutes. Drain and put in a large bowl. Add the butternut squash, tomatoes and garlic. Season generously and add 3 tbs of olive oil. Stir to evenly coat the vegetables.

Place on a baking tray and roast for 30 minutes. Turn the vegetables over and continue to roast for 10 minutes or until all the vegetables are soft, have browned and become crisp on the edges, and the tomatoes have reduced to a sauce.

CHAPTER FIVE
GRATINS

95 Ricotta and cherry tomato sformato

500g Ricotta • 350g Cherry tomatoes • 1 Garlic clove, peeled and cut in half • 6 Eggs • 200ml Crème fraîche • 2 tbs Thyme leaves • Butter for greasing the dish • 50g Parmesan, freshly grated • Extra virgin olive oil

Preheat the oven to 200°C/Gas Mark 6.

Toss the tomatoes with the garlic and 1 tbs of olive oil, then season. Place in a small baking dish and bake for 15 minutes.

Beat the ricotta in a food mixer, then add the eggs one by one and beat until light. Put this mixture in a bowl, add the crème fraîche and stir together. Season and add half the thyme.

Butter an ovenproof dish, 36 x 24cm, then dust the dish with the Parmesan. Spoon in the ricotta mixture, scatter over the tomatoes with their juices and the remaining thyme. Drizzle with olive oil and bake for 20 minutes. Serve warm.

96 Ricotta and chard on pasta frolla

200g Ricotta • 750g Swiss chard leaves, with their stalks, chopped • 1 Red onion, peeled and sliced • 1 Garlic clove, peeled and sliced • 3 tbs Thyme leaves • 2 tbs Crème fraîche • 1 Egg yolk •

100g Parmesan, freshly grated • 50g Small black olives, stoned • Extra virgin olive oil

Pasta frolla (flaky pastry)
360g Plain flour • 225g Unsalted butter, very cold, cut into 1cm cubes • 1 tsp Sea salt • 6 tbs Iced water

Put the flour, butter and salt into a food processor and pulse-chop to the consistency of breadcrumbs. Add the iced water and pulse for 1 second to combine. Gather the dough into a ball, wrap in cling film and refrigerate for 1 hour.

Preheat the oven to 200°C/Gas Mark 6.

Cook the chard in boiling salted water for 8 minutes, then drain.

Heat 2 tbs of olive oil in a thick-bottomed frying pan. Fry the onion until soft and light brown. Add the garlic and fry until soft, then add the thyme. Cook briefly to combine the flavours. Add the chard, mix well and remove from the heat. Season.

Beat the ricotta with a fork and season. Separately mix the crème fraîche with the egg yolk and half the Parmesan.

Coarsely grate the pastry onto a large, flat baking tray. Press out to cover the whole surface as thinly as possible. The edges can be thicker. Bake for 10 minutes. Cover the pastry with the chard mixture, dot with the ricotta and pour over the crème fraîche. Add the olives and drizzle with olive oil. Scatter over the remaining Parmesan and return to the oven for 10-15 minutes. Serve hot, cut into squares.

Ricotta and chard on pasta frolla (Recipe 96)

97   Pea and mint sformato

2kg Peas in the pod, shelled • 3 tbs Mint leaves, half of them chopped • 75g Unsalted butter • 150g Parmesan, freshly grated • 200g Spring onions, peeled and finely chopped • 3 tbs Basil leaves, half of them chopped • 250g Ricotta • 3 tbs Double cream • 3 Eggs • Extra virgin olive oil

Preheat the oven to 190°C/Gas Mark 5.

Butter a 25cm spring-release baking tin and line it with baking parchment. Dust with some of the Parmesan.

Melt the remaining butter in a thick-bottomed pan, add the spring onions and fry gently until soft. Add the peas and the whole mint and basil leaves and cook for a minute. Add 100ml hot water, cover and simmer for 5 minutes. Remove from the heat and cool.

Put half the ricotta and half the pea mixture in a food processor, add half the cream and blend to mix briefly. Add the rest of the ricotta and the eggs one by one, finally adding the remaining cream. Pour this mixture into a bowl, add the remaining peas and the chopped mint and basil and stir in the remaining Parmesan.

Pour into the prepared tin and drizzle with olive oil. Bake for 30 minutes, until the sformato is firm and brown on top and the edges are coming away from the side of the tin. Cool for 5 minutes. Remove from the tin to a serving dish. Serve at room temperature, cut into wedges.

98 Jerusalem artichoke gratin with cream and Parmesan

1kg Jerusalem artichokes • 100ml Double cream • 120g Parmesan, freshly grated • Juice of 1 lemon • 4 Garlic cloves, peeled • 3 tbs Thyme leaves • 1 Dried red chilli, crumbled • 80g Unsalted butter • 150ml Chicken stock

Preheat the oven to 200°C/Gas Mark 6.

Peel the artichokes and cut them into 1cm slices. Put them into a bowl of cold water containing the lemon juice as you work. Crush the garlic and thyme with 1 tsp of sea salt until it becomes a fine paste. Add 2 tbs of water to the paste to loosen.

Drain the artichokes and pat dry. Put in a bowl and mix in the garlic paste. Add the chilli and some black pepper and a little sea salt.

Generously butter a large ovenproof dish. Shake over half the Parmesan so that it sticks to the butter. Place the artichokes in the dish. Scatter over half the remaining Parmesan and add the chicken stock. Dot with a little butter. Cover with foil and bake for 20 minutes. Remove the foil and add the cream, sprinkle over the remaining Parmesan and dot with the remaining butter. Bake for a further 10 minutes, until the liquid has thickened and the top is crisp and brown.

99 Potato and fennel gratin

600g Waxy potatoes, peeled • 600g Fennel bulbs, tough outer layers and stalks removed (chop the green leafy tops) • ½ Ciabatta loaf, crust removed • 100g Parmesan, freshly grated • 6 Garlic cloves, peeled • Juice of 1 lemon • 250ml Double cream • 80g Unsalted butter

Preheat the oven to 200°C/Gas Mark 6.

Cut each fennel bulb in half lengthways, then each half into 4. Cut the potatoes in half lengthways and then in half again lengthways. The pieces of fennel and potato should be similar in size.

Pulse-chop the ciabatta to coarse breadcrumbs in a food processor. Combine the breadcrumbs with 2 tbs of the Parmesan and the fennel tops.

Place the fennel and potatoes in salted boiling water with the garlic cloves and lemon juice and cook for 8 minutes. Remove the fennel and potatoes and place in a bowl, leaving the garlic in the water.

Drain off half the water. Add the cream and bring to the boil. Simmer until it thickens. Mash the garlic into the cream and add the remaining Parmesan. Add the cream mixture to the potatoes and fennel, mix well and season.

Butter a baking dish and pour in the potato mixture. Dot with half the butter and bake for 30 minutes. Sprinkle over the breadcrumbs and dot with the remaining butter. Return to the oven and bake until crisp and brown.

100 Potato, trevise, pancetta and sage gratin

750g Waxy potatoes, peeled and cut into slices 5mm thick • 3 Trevise heads • 100g Pancetta, thinly sliced • 20 Sage leaves • 3 Garlic cloves, peeled and finely sliced • 50g Parmesan, freshly grated • Extra virgin olive oil

Preheat the oven to 180°C/Gas Mark 4.

Heat 1 tbs of olive oil in a thick-bottomed frying pan and gently fry the pancetta with the sage and garlic for 3 minutes.

Peel and chop the trevise stalks; chop the leaves. Mix with 2 tbs of olive oil and season.

Rinse the potatoes in cold water, then place in a large bowl. Add the pancetta, sage and garlic and their juices. Toss together and mix in the trevise.

Place the potato mixture in an ovenproof dish, drizzle with olive oil and cover with foil. Seal tightly and bake for 30 minutes. Remove the foil, sprinkle with the Parmesan and return to the oven. Increase the temperature to 200°C/Gas Mark 6 and bake for 10 minutes, or until the potatoes are soft and the surface brown.

Potato, trevise, pancetta and sage gratin (Recipe 100)

101 Potato and pancetta gratin

*500g Waxy potatoes, peeled and cut into slices
5mm thick • 100g Pancetta, thinly sliced • 2 Garlic
cloves, peeled and thinly sliced • 10 Sage leaves •
200ml Double cream • 50g Parmesan, freshly grated •
Extra virgin olive oil*

Preheat the oven to 200°C/Gas Mark 6.

Heat 3 tbs of olive oil in a thick-bottomed frying pan
and add the pancetta, garlic and sage. Gently fry until
the garlic is soft and the pancetta translucent.

Rinse the potato slices in cold water, then place them
in a large bowl and add the pancetta mixture. Toss
together and add the cream. Season. Put the potato
mixture into a baking dish, cover with foil and bake for
30 minutes.

Remove the foil, scatter with the Parmesan, drizzle with
olive oil and return to the oven for 10 minutes or until
the potatoes are soft and browned at the edges.

102 Swiss chard gratin

*1kg Swiss chard leaves, with their stalks • 2 Thyme
sprigs • 2 Bay leaves • 3 tbs Red wine vinegar •
100g Unsalted butter • 1 Red onion, peeled and finely
sliced • 2 Garlic cloves, peeled and sliced • 10 Anchovy
fillets • 1 Dried red chilli, crumbled • 1 tbs Plain flour •
1/2 Nutmeg, freshly grated • 75g Parmesan, freshly
grated • 50g Black olives, stoned*

Preheat the oven to 200°C/Gas Mark 6.

Cut the stalks from the chard leaves. Trim the fibrous edges of the stalks and cut into 1cm pieces. Cook the chard leaves in boiling salted water for 5 minutes, then remove with a slotted spoon. Lay out to cool. Add the thyme, bay leaves and vinegar to the boiling water. Add the chard stalks and cook for 6 minutes. Drain, keeping the cooking water. Discard the thyme and bay.

Melt $2/3$ of the butter in a thick-bottomed pan, add the onion and fry until soft and beginning to colour. Add the garlic and cook for 2 minutes. Add the anchovies and stir them constantly until they melt into the butter. Season with black pepper and the chilli. Add the flour, stir, then cook over a low heat for 8 minutes.

Spoonful by spoonful, add the cooking water, stirring constantly until you have a sauce the consistency of double cream. Season with black pepper and nutmeg. Add the stalks and check the seasoning.

Butter an ovenproof china dish. Spread a layer of stalks and sauce in it and cover with chard leaves. Dot with butter and sprinkle with half the Parmesan. Spread a second layer of sauce over and cover with chard leaves. Dot with more butter, scatter with the olives and drizzle with any remaining sauce. Sprinkle with the remaining Parmesan. Bake for 20 minutes, until lightly browned on top.

Swiss chard gratin (Recipe 102)

CHAPTER SIX
FRIED VEGETABLES

103 Zucchini fritti

1 kg Zucchini • 2 litres Sunflower oil for frying

Batter
150g Plain flour • 3 tbs Warm water •
3 Egg whites • Extra virgin olive oil

Cut the zucchini into 5mm discs, then cut each disc into 5mm-thick matchsticks. Place in a colander, sprinkle with sea salt and leave for 30 minutes. Pat dry.

For the batter, sift the flour into a medium bowl and make a well in the centre. Pour in 3 tbs of olive oil and stir slowly, combining the flour with the oil. Slowly add the warm water to loosen this paste, stirring all the time, until you have a batter the consistency of double cream. Leave for a minimum of 45 minutes.

Heat the sunflower oil to 190°C in a high-sided pan. Beat the egg whites until stiff and fold gently into the batter.

Dip the zucchini in the batter, then fry in batches in the hot oil until golden and crisp. Drain on kitchen paper, season and serve immediately.

104 Zucchini scapece, Pugliese style

1 kg Zucchini • 2 litres Sunflower oil for frying •
3 tbs Mint leaves • 3 tbs Red wine vinegar • 2 Garlic
cloves, peeled and sliced into very fine slivers • 2 Dried
red chillies, crumbled

Cut the zucchini into discs 5mm thick, then cut each disc into 5mm-thick matchsticks. Place in a colander, sprinkle with sea salt and leave for 30 minutes. Pat dry.

Heat the sunflower oil to 190°C in a high-sided pan. Fry the zucchini in batches until light brown. Drain on kitchen paper. Fry the mint leaves for 2 seconds only. Drain.

Place the zucchini on a flat dish and sprinkle with the vinegar, then scatter with the garlic slices and mint leaves. Season with sea salt and the chilli.

105 Zucchini scapece

*1kg Zucchini • 2 litres Sunflower oil for frying •
2 tbs Red wine vinegar • 2 Garlic cloves, peeled and
sliced into very fine slivers • 1 Fresh red chilli, cut in
half lengthways, de-seeded and cut into fine slivers •
2 tbs Mint leaves*

Thinly slice the zucchini into discs; the thinner they are, the crisper they will be when fried. Place in a large bowl of iced water for 30 minutes. Drain and pat dry.

Heat the sunflower oil to 180°C in a high-sided pan. Fry the zucchini in batches until light brown and crisp. Drain on kitchen paper.

Place the zucchini on a large, flat plate and sprinkle over the vinegar, then scatter over the garlic and chilli. Tear the mint leaves and scatter them over. Season and serve at room temperature.

Zucchini scapece (Recipe 105)

106 Fried aubergine with tomato and basil

2 Aubergines, sliced 3mm thick • 6 Plum tomatoes, skinned and roughly chopped • 3 tbs Basil leaves • 2 Garlic cloves, peeled and sliced • 300ml Sunflower oil • 3 tbs Red wine vinegar • Extra virgin olive oil

Lay the aubergines on kitchen paper, sprinkle with sea salt and leave for 30 minutes.

Heat 2 tbs of olive oil in a thick-bottomed pan, add the garlic and let it colour. Add half the basil, plus the tomatoes and 1 tsp of sea salt. Cook for 15 minutes, until you have a thickish sauce.

Wash the salt off the aubergines and pat dry. Heat half the sunflower oil in a large, flat frying pan. When it is very hot, place a layer of aubergine slices in the pan and fry briefly on each side until golden and crisp on the edges. Drain on kitchen paper. Continue frying the aubergines, adding more oil to the pan if necessary.

To serve, lay the aubergines on a large, flat plate and sprinkle with the vinegar. Spoon the tomato sauce over, but not completely covering the aubergines. Scatter over the remaining basil. Serve at room temperature.

107 Fritto misto

Batter (see Recipe 103) • 8 Zucchini flowers, with their stalks attached (the male flowers) • 1 Aubergine, sliced into 5mm discs • 250g Zucchini, sliced into 5mm discs, then into 5mm matchsticks • 8 Anchovy fillets • 16 Large sage leaves • Flour for dusting • 2 litres Sunflower oil for frying • 2 Lemons, halved

Make the batter and leave for 45 minutes.

To prepare the flowers, remove the stamens and the green sepals at the base of each one.

Lay the aubergine and zucchini on kitchen paper. Sprinkle with sea salt and leave for 30 minutes. Rinse and pat dry.

Place each anchovy fillet between 2 sage leaves and press to hold together. The oiliness of the anchovy will help the sage to stick. Dust with plain flour.

Heat the sunflower oil to 180°C in a high-sided pan. Beat the egg whites for the batter until stiff. Fold them into the batter.

Dip the zucchini, aubergine and zucchini flowers into the batter and tap gently to knock off excess. Fry in batches until golden brown and crisp. Drain on kitchen paper.

Fry the anchovy and sage directly in the oil without any batter.

Serve a selection, scattered with sea salt, with the lemon halves.

Fritto misto (Recipe 107)

108 Deep-fried zucchini flowers

20 Zucchini flowers, with their stalks attached (the male flowers) • Batter (see Recipe 103) • 2 litres Sunflower oil for frying • 2 Lemons, halved

Make the batter and leave for 45 minutes.

To prepare the flowers, remove the stamens and the green sepals at the base of each one.

Fill a large frying pan 1.5cm deep with sunflower oil. Heat the oil to 180°C. Beat the egg whites for the batter until stiff, then fold them into the batter.

Dip the flowers into the batter one at a time. Tap gently to knock off the excess. Place 3 or 4 flowers in the hot oil, fry until crisp and golden, then turn them over and crisp the other side. Drain on kitchen paper. Serve with the lemon halves.

109 Fried zucchini flowers stuffed with basil and ricotta

20 Zucchini flowers, with their stalks attached (the male flowers) • 2 tbs Basil leaves • 250g Ricotta • Batter (see Recipe 103) • 2 litres Sunflower oil for fryiing • 2 Lemons, halved

Make the batter and leave for 45 minutes.

To prepare the flowers, remove the stamens and the green sepals at the base of each one. Season the ricotta. Push a teaspoon of ricotta and a basil leaf inside each flower. Press the petals together.

Fill a large frying pan 1.5cm deep with sunflower oil. Heat the oil to 180°C. Beat the egg whites for the batter until stiff. Fold them into the batter.

Dip the flowers into the batter one at a time. Tap gently to knock off any excess. Place 3 or 4 flowers in the oil, fry until crisp and golden, then turn them over and crisp the other side. Drain on kitchen paper. Serve with the lemons.

110 Fried porcini with parsley and garlic

1kg Fresh porcini mushrooms, wiped clean with a damp cloth • 2 tbs Chopped flat-leaf parsley • 4 Garlic cloves, peeled and finely chopped • Bruschetta, to serve (see Recipe 18) • Extra virgin olive oil

Separate the mushroom caps from the stalks. Chop the stalks and slice the caps into 1cm pieces. Heat a large, thick-bottomed frying pan and add 2 tbs of olive oil. When very hot, add the stalks and shake the pan over a high heat until they are beginning to colour. Then add the sliced caps and continue to fry until they are golden. Lower the heat, add the parsley and garlic and fry for 5-6 minutes. Season and serve with the bruschetta.

Fried porcini with parsley and garlic (Recipe 110)

111 Fritto misto da Delfino

Batter (see Recipe 103) • 8 Zucchini flowers, with stalks attached • 8 Marigold flower buds, with stalks and leaves • 8 Borrage flowerheads, with stalks and leaves • 8 Pumpkin plant shoots, with flowerbuds, stalks and leaves • 8 Large sage leaves • 4 Baby artichokes, peeled and cut into quarters • 2 litres Sunflower oil for frying • 2 Lemons, halved

Make the batter and leave for 45 minutes.

To prepare the zucchini flowers, remove the stamens and the green sepals at the base of each one. Trim the tough stalks from the marigolds and borrage.

Fill a large frying pan 1cm deep with sunflower oil. Heat the oil to 180°C. Dip the different flowers, leaves and shoots into the batter, and tap gently to knock off any excess. Fry in batches until golden brown and crisp. Drain on kitchen paper.

Serve a selection scattered with sea salt, with the lemon halves.

Carciofi alla giuda

4 Large Romanesco artichokes • 2 litres Sunflower oil for frying • 1 Lemon, cut into quarters

Pull the tough outer leaves off the artichokes and trim the stalks to 2cm from the base.

Heat the oil to 100°C in a high-sided saucepan. Fry the artichokes, one at a time, for 15 minutes, pushing them down so they are covered by the hot oil. Drain on kitchen paper and allow to cool.

Peel away a further layer of only the toughest leaves and peel the fibres from the stalk. Gently prise open each artichoke.

Increase the temperature of the oil to 170°C. Fry each artichoke a second time for about 2-3 minutes, until the leaves become brownish and crisp. Drain, stalk-side up, on kitchen paper. Whilst still hot, place on a plate, still stalk-side up, and place another plate on top. Press down to flatten the artichokes and to squeeze out excess oil. Some leaves may come off. Scatter each artichoke with sea salt and serve with the lemon quarters.

Carciofi alla giuda (Recipe 112)

CHAPTER SEVEN
BOILED
VEGETABLES

113 Asparagus with anchovy butter

*1kg Asparagus, tough ends snapped off • 6 Anchovy
fillets, roughly chopped • 150g Unsalted butter,
softened • Juice of 1 lemon • 50g Parmesan shavings •
Extra virgin olive oil*

Mix the anchovies with the lemon juice and some
black pepper in a bowl. Mix in the butter with a fork.

Cook the asparagus in boiling salted water until
tender, then drain. Place in a bowl, season and drizzle
with olive oil.

Serve on warm plates with the anchovy butter and a
few shavings of Parmesan placed on top.

114 Artichokes with olive oil and fresh chilli

*8 Globe artichokes • 2 Fresh red chillies • 3 Bay
leaves • 3 Thyme sprigs • 3 Garlic cloves, peeled •
115ml Red wine vinegar • 1 Lemon, cut into
quarters • Extra virgin olive oil*

Pull the tough outer leaves off the artichokes and trim
the stalks to 2cm. Put the artichokes in a small
saucepan so they fit tightly together. Pour in enough
cold water just to cover the artichokes and add the
bay, thyme, whole chillies and garlic. Add the vinegar,
4 tbs of olive oil and 1 tbs of sea salt. Cover the pan,
bring to the boil and simmer gently for 20 minutes or

until the artichokes are tender. Remove from the heat and cool in the cooking water.

When cool, take the artichokes out, keeping the cooking liquid, herbs and chillies. Pull off any remaining tough leaves, testing by bite. Peel the stalks and cut off the tough top tips of the leaves.

Place the artichokes in a serving bowl. Spoon off the oily part of the cooking liquid and pour over the artichokes. Discard the remaining liquid. Split open the chillies and place them and the herb leaves amongst the artichokes. Season and pour over 3 tbs of olive oil. Serve at room temperature, with the lemon quarters.

115 Castelluccio lentils with herbs

*200g Castelluccio lentils • 2 Garlic cloves, peeled •
3 Sage leaves • Choose 3 or more of the following
herbs: 1 tbs Mint, 1 tbs Parsley, 1 tbs Marjoram, 1 tbs
Basil, 1 tbs Oregano • Extra virgin olive oil*

Rinse the lentils under cold water. Put in a small saucepan with the garlic and sage. Cover with cold water, bring to the boil and simmer gently for 20 minutes, or until the lentils are al dente.

Drain, discarding the garlic and sage. Add 3 tbs of olive oil, season and mix well. Roughly chop the herbs together and add to the lentils. Serve warm.

Castelluccio lentils with herbs (Recipe 115)

116 Samphire with olive oil and lemon

*1.5kg Samphire, tough stems removed, washed twice •
Juice of 1 lemon, plus 1 lemon cut into quarters • Extra
virgin olive oil*

Cook the samphire in boiling salted water for 6-8
minutes, until tender. Drain and season, if necessary,
with salt and plenty of black pepper. Pour over 3 tbs
of olive oil and the lemon juice and toss. Serve warm,
with the lemon quarters.

117 Swiss chard with olive oil and lemon

*1kg Swiss chard leaves, with their stalks • Juice of
1 lemon • Extra virgin olive oil*

Cut the Swiss chard leaves off the stalks, trim the
edges of the stalks and cut into pieces 1 cm thick.

Cook the stalks in boiling salted water for 5 minutes or
until tender. Remove from the water with a slotted
spoon and drain. Cook the leaves in the same water for
5 minutes. Drain and roughly chop. Mix with the stalks.

Put the lemon juice in a bowl, add 4 times its volume
of olive oil and season. Pour this dressing over the
chard and toss. Serve at room temperature.

118 Peas sott'olio with mint

2kg Fresh peas in the pod, shelled • 3 tbs Mint leaves • Extra virgin olive oil

Cook the peas in boiling salted water for 4 minutes, adding the mint for the final minute. Drain and put into a serving bowl. Season. Pour 150ml olive oil over the hot peas. Serve hot or at room temperature.

119 Swiss chard with lentils and herbs

1kg Swiss chard leaves, with their stalks, roughly chopped • Castelluccio lentils with herbs (see Recipe 115) • 1 Garlic clove, peeled and sliced • 2 tbs Roughly chopped flat-leaf parsley • 1 Dried red chilli, crumbled • Extra virgin olive oil

Cook the chard leaves and stalks together in boiling salted water for about 5 minutes or until soft. Drain.

Heat 2 tbs of olive oil in a thick-bottomed frying pan. Add the garlic and parsley and cook until the garlic is soft and golden. Add the chard and chilli and cook briefly to combine the flavours. Season. Stir in the lentils and add 1 tbs of olive oil. Cook just to heat up the lentils. Serve warm.

120 Green beans and tomatoes

500g Green beans, stems removed • 350g Ripe tomatoes, skinned and roughly chopped • 2 Garlic cloves, peeled and finely sliced • 2 tbs Basil leaves • Extra virgin olive oil

Heat 2 tbs of olive oil in a thick-bottomed pan. Add the garlic and cook until soft and golden. Add the tomatoes and half the basil, season, and cook for 15 minutes to reduce to a sauce.

Cook the beans in boiling salted water for 8-10 minutes, until tender. Drain and add to the tomato sauce. Stir to combine, add the remaining basil and drizzle with olive oil.

121 Mashed potatoes with green beans

500g New potatoes, skin scrubbed away • 500g Green beans, stems removed • 2 Garlic cloves, peeled and cut in half lengthways • 2 tbs Chopped flat-leaf parsley • Extra virgin olive oil

Put the potatoes in a small pan with cold water to cover and 1 tsp of salt and bring to the boil. Simmer for 15-20 minutes or until tender. Drain. Mash the potatoes roughly with a fork, mix in 2 tbs of olive oil and season.

Cook the green beans with the garlic in boiling salted water for 8-10 minutes, until tender. Drain. Smash the beans with the garlic and add the parsley and 1 tbs of olive oil.

Combine the potatoes and beans. Season. Drizzle over a little more olive oil and serve warm.

122 Chickpeas with potatoes

100g Dried chickpeas, soaked in cold water with 1 tsp bicarbonate of soda for 24 hours • 500g Waxy potatoes, peeled • 1 Fresh red chilli • 3 Garlic cloves, peeled • 1 Celery heart, outside green stalks removed, cut in half • 3 Plum tomatoes, halved • Juice of 1 lemon • Extra virgin olive oil

Rinse the chickpeas and put them in a thick-bottomed pan. Add 2 potatoes, the whole chilli, garlic, celery heart and tomatoes. Cover with cold water and bring to the boil. Turn the heat down, skim the surface and simmer for 45 minutes or until the chickpeas are tender. Drain.

Remove the chilli, peel the skin, and return the pulp and seeds to the chickpeas. Remove the tomato skin. Mash the celery heart, garlic and potatoes into the chickpeas. Season and stir in 3 tbs of olive oil.

Cook the remaining potatoes in boiling salted water until soft. Drain and roughly chop. Add to the chickpeas and mix to combine all the vegetables. Add a further 2 tbs of olive oil. Place in a serving dish.

Chickpeas with potatoes (Recipe 122)

123 Half-mashed potato with parsley

750g Waxy potatoes, peeled and cut into equal-sized pieces • 4 tbs Finely chopped flat-leaf parsley • 4 Garlic cloves, peeled • Extra virgin olive oil

Put the potatoes in a thick-bottomed pan with the garlic. Cover with cold water, add 1 tsp of sea salt and cook for 20 minutes or until soft. Drain and season whilst hot. Return to the pan. Add 100ml of olive oil and the parsley. Stir them in the saucepan, breaking the potatoes into a mash.

124 Agretti

*750g Agretti, trimmed of the tough red stalk • Juice of
½ lemon • Extra virgin olive oil*

Cook the agretti in boiling salted water for 4 minutes.
Drain and season while still hot. Add 4 tbs of olive oil
and the lemon juice and toss. Serve warm.

*Agretti, otherwise known as Barba di frate or Monk's
beard, is found in all the northern markets in Italy in the
spring. Although not always available here, it is easy to
grow from seed. Agretti has a salty, earthy spinach
flavour and grows in bunches with chive-like leaves.*

125 Peas and broad beans sott'olio

*1kg Peas in the pod, shelled • 1kg Young broad beans
in the pod, shelled • 1 Garlic clove, peeled • 1 tbs Mint
leaves • 2 tbs Basil leaves • Extra virgin olive oil*

Cook the broad beans with the clove of garlic in
boiling water for 3 minutes. Add the mint and continue
boiling for 1 minute. Drain and lightly mash with a fork
while hot. Season and stir in 2 tbs of olive oil.

Cook the peas in boiling salted water for 3 minutes,
then drain. Immediately pour over 2 tbs of olive oil.
Leave to cool. Mix the peas into the broad bean
mixture. Chop the basil and stir it into the mixture.
Serve at room temperature.

Peas and broad beans sott'olio (Recipe 125)

Index

The authors would like to thank Tanya Nathan, Ronnie Bonnetti, Fiona MacIntyre, Imogen Fortes, Sarah Lavelle, David Loftus and Mark Porter, and all the staff at the River Cafe.

1 3 5 7 9 10 8 6 4 2

Text © Rose Gray and Ruth Rogers 2006

Rose Gray and Ruth Rogers have asserted their moral right to be identified as the authors of this work in accordance with the Copyright, Design and Patents Act 1988.

First published in the United Kingdom in 2006 by Ebury Press, an imprint of Ebury Publishing, Random House UK Ltd., 20 Vauxhall Bridge Road, London SW1V 2SA

Random House Australia (Pty) Limited, 20 Alfred Street, Milsons Point, Sydney, New South Wales 2061, Australia

Random House New Zealand Limited, 18 Poland Road, Glenfield, Auckland 10, New Zealand

Random House (Pty) Limited, Isle of Houghton Corner of Boundary Road & Carse O'Gowrie Houghton, 2198, South Africa

Random House Publishers India Private Limited, 301 World Trade Tower, Hotel Intercontinental Grand Complex, Barakhamba Lane, New Delhi 110 001, India

Random House UK Limited Reg. No. 954009, www.randomhouse.co.uk

Papers used by Ebury Press are natural, recyclable products made from wood grown in sustainable forests.

A CIP catalogue record is available for this book from the British Library.

ISBN: 009191437X   ISBN: 9780091914370 (from Jan 2007)

Printed and bound in Italy by Graphicom SRL

Designed by Mark Porter Design, www.markporter.com

Copies are available at special rates for bulk orders. Contact the sales development team on 020 7840 8487 or visit www.booksforpromotions.co.uk for more information.